KEIGHLEY COLLEGE LIB
TEL: 01535 618519

KT-177-427

To renew
on        94

-6. MAR. 1996

ode number

-8. JUN.

994

24. MAY 1996

udying society:
sociological theories
and research practices

KEIGHLEY CAMPUS LIBRARY
LEEDS CITY COLLEGE

KC08517

*For Effie, from Pip*

# Studying society: sociological theories and research practices

PHILIP JONES

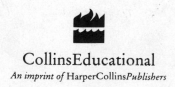

CollinsEducational

*An imprint of* HarperCollins*Publishers*

© Philip Jones, 1993

This book is copyright under the Berne Convention.

No reproduction without permission. All rights reserved.

The author asserts the moral right to be identified as the author of this work.

Published by
**CollinsEducational**
77-85 Fulham Palace Road
Hammersmith
London W6 8JB

First published in 1993

Typeset in 10 on 12 Palatino by CG Graphic Services, Aylesbury
and printed and bound by HarperCollinsManufacturing, Glasgow.

KEIGHLEY COLLEGE
LIBRARY

43598 93/94

7 FEB 1994    HW

# Contents

Contents

# CHAPTER ONE

# *An introduction to sociological theories*

Humans are social beings. Whether we like it or not, nearly everything we do in our lives takes place in the company of others. Few of our activities are truly solitary, scarce are the times when we are really alone. Thus the study of how we are able to interact with one another, and what happens when we do, would seem to be one of the most fundamental concerns of anyone interested in human life.

Yet strangely enough, it was not until relatively recently – from about the beginning of the nineteenth century onwards – that a specialist interest in this intrinsically *social* aspect of human existence was treated with any seriousness. Before that time, and even since, other kinds of interests have dominated the analysis of human life. Two of the most resilient, non-social approaches to human behaviour have been 'naturalistic' and 'individualistic' explanations.

Rather than seeing social behaviour as the product of interaction, these theories have concentrated on the presumed qualities inherent in individuals. On the one hand, naturalistic explanations suppose that all human behaviour – social interaction included – is a product of the inherited dispositions we possess as animals. We are, like animals, biologically programmed by nature. On the other hand, individualistic explanations baulk at such grand generalisations about the inevitability of behaviour. From this point of view we are all 'individual' and 'different'. Explanations of human behaviour must therefore always rest ultimately on the particular and unique psychological qualities of individuals.

Sociological theories are in direct contrast to these 'non-social' approaches. Looking a little closer at them, and discovering what is wrong or incomplete about them, makes it easier to understand why sociological theories exist.

NATURALISTIC THEORIES

Naturalistic explanations of human activity are common enough. For example, in our society it is often argued that it is only natural for a man and a woman to fall in love, get married and have children. It is equally natural for this nuclear family to live as a unit on their own, with the husband going out to work to earn resources for his dependants, while his wife, at least for the early years of her children's lives, devotes herself to looking after them – to being a mother. As they grow up and acquire more independence, it is still only 'natural' for the children to live at home with their parents, who are responsible for them, at least until their late teens. By then it is only natural for them to want to 'leave the nest', to start to 'make their own way in the world' and, in particular, to look for marriage partners. Thus they, too, can start families of their own.

The corollary of these 'natural' practices is that it is somehow *unnatural not* to want to get married, or to marry for reasons other than love. It is equally unnatural for a couple *not* to want to have children, or for wives *not* to want to be mothers, or for mothers *not* to want to devote the whole of their lives to child-rearing. Though it is not right or natural for children to leave home much younger than 18, it is certainly not natural for them not to want to leave home at all in order to start a family of their own.

However, these 'unnatural' desires and practices are common enough in our society. There are plenty of people who prefer to stay single, or 'marry with an eye on the main chance'. There are plenty of women who do not like the idea of motherhood, and there is certainly any number of women who do not want to spend their lives solely being wives and mothers. There are plenty of children who want to leave home long before they are 18 while there are many who are quite happy to stay as members of their parents' households until long after that age.

Why is this? If human behaviour is, in fact, the product of a disposition inherent in the nature of the human being then why are such deviations from what is 'natural' so common? We can hardly put down the widespread existence of such 'unnatural' patterns of behaviour to some kind of large-scale, faulty genetic programming!

In any case, why are there so many variations from these notions of 'normal' family practices in other kinds of human societies? Both history and anthropology provide us with stark contrasts in family life. In his book on family life in Medieval Europe, *Centuries of Childhood* (1973), Philippe Ariès paints a picture of marriage, the family and child-rearing which sharply contradicts our notions of normality. Families were not then, as they are for us today, private and isolated units, cut off socially, and physically separated from the world at large. Families were deeply

2

embedded in the community, with people living essentially public, rather than private, lives. They lived in households whose composition was constantly shifting; relatives, friends, children, visitors, passers-by and animals all slept under the same roof. Marriage was primarily a means of forging alliances rather than simply the outcome of 'love', while women certainly did not look upon mothering as their sole destiny. Indeed, child-rearing was a far less demanding and onerous task than it is in our world. Children were not cosseted and coddled to anywhere near the extent we consider 'right'. Many more people – both other relatives and the community at large – were involved in child-rearing, and childhood lasted a far shorter time than it does today. As Ariès (1973) puts it '. . . as soon as he had been weaned, or soon after, the child became the natural companion of the adult.'

In contemporary non-industrial societies too, there is a wide range of variations in family practices. Here again, marriage is essentially a means of establishing alliances between groups, rather than simply a relationship between individuals. Monogamy – one husband and one wife – is only one form of marriage. Polygyny – marriage between a husband and more than one wife – and polyandry – between a wife and more than one husband – are found in many societies. Domestic life is also far more public and communal than it is in industrial societies. Each family unit is just a part of a much wider, cooperating, group of mainly blood relatives associated with a local territory, usually a village. As in Medieval Europe, therefore, child-rearing is not considered the principal responsibility of parents alone, but involves a far greater number of people, relatives and non-relatives.

Clearly, then, to hope to explain human life simply by reference to natural impulses common to all is to ignore the one crucial fact that sociology directs attention to: human behaviour varies according to the *social* settings in which people find themselves.


INDIVIDUALISTIC THEORIES

What of individualistic explanations? How useful is the argument that behaviour is the product of the psychological make-up of individuals? The employment of this kind of theory is extremely common. For example, success or failure in *education* is often assumed to be merely a reflection of intelligence: bright children succeed and dim children fail. *Criminals* are often taken to be people with certain kinds of personality; they are usually seen as morally deficient individuals, lacking any real sense of right or wrong. *Unemployed* people are equally often condemned as 'work-shy', 'lazy' or 'scroungers' – inadequates who would rather 'get something for nothing' than work for it. *Suicide* is seen as the act of an unstable person – an act undertaken when, as coroners put it, 'the balance of the mind was disturbed'. This kind of explanation is attractive for many people and has proved particularly resilient to sociological critique. But a closer look shows it to be seriously flawed.

If educational achievement is simply a reflection of intelligence then why do children from manual workers' homes do so badly compared with children from middle-class homes? It is clearly nonsensical to suggest that doing one kind of job rather than another is likely to determine the *intelligence* of your child. Achievement in education must in some way be influenced by the characteristics of a child's background.

Equally, the fact that the majority of people convicted of a crime come from certain social categories must cast serious doubt on the 'deficient personality' theory. The conviction rate is highest for young males, especially Blacks, who come from manual, working-class or unemployed backgrounds. Can we seriously believe that criminal *personalities* are likely to be concentrated in such *social* categories? As in the case of educational achievement, it is clear that the conviction of criminals must somehow be influenced by social factors.

Again, is it likely that the three million or so people presently unemployed are typically uninterested in working when the vast majority of them have been forced out of their jobs by the recession – through a collection of social forces quite outside their control?

Suicide would seem to have the strongest case for being explained as a purely psychological act. But if it is simply a question of 'an unsound mind', then why does the rate of suicide vary between societies? Why does it vary between different groups within the same society? Also, why do the rates in groups and societies remain remarkably constant over time? As in other examples, social factors must be exerting some kind of influence; explanations at the level of the personality are clearly not enough.

Variations such as these demonstrate the inadequacy of theories of human behaviour which exclusively emphasise innate natural drives, or the unique psychological make-up of individuals. If nature is at the root of behaviour, why does it vary according to social settings? If we are all different individuals acting according to the dictates of unique psychological influences, why do different people in the same social circumstances behave similarly and in ways others can understand? Clearly there is a *social* dimension to human existence which requires *sociological* theorising to explain it.

All sociological theories thus have in common an emphasis on the way human belief and action is the product of social influences. They differ as to what these influences are, and how they should be investigated and explained. This book is about these differences.

We shall now examine three distinct kinds of theory – *consensus*, *conflict* and *action* theories – each of which highlights specific social sources of human behaviour. Though virtually none of the sociologists whose work we will spend the rest of the book examining falls neatly into any one of these three categories of theory, discussing them now will produce two benefits:

(1) to serve as an accessible introduction to theoretical debates in sociology and;
(2) to act as useful reference points against which to judge and compare the work of the subject's major theorists.

*Society as a structure of rules – the influence of culture on behaviour*

Imagine you live in a big city. How many people do you know well? Twenty? Fifty? A hundred? Now consider how many other people you encounter each day, about whom you know *nothing*. For example, how many complete strangers do people living in London or Manchester or Birmingham come into contact with each day? On the street, in shops, on buses and trains, in cinemas or night clubs – everyday life in a big city is a constant encounter with complete strangers. Yet even if city dwellers bothered to reflect on this fact, they would not normally leave their homes quaking with dread about how all these hundreds of strangers would behave towards them. Indeed, they hardly, if ever, think about it. Why? Why do we take our ability to cope with strangers so much for granted? It is because nearly all the people we encounter in our everyday lives do behave in ways we expect. We *expect* bus passengers, shoppers, taxi-drivers, passers-by, and so on, to behave in quite definite ways even though we know nothing about them *personally*. City dwellers in particular – though it is true of all of us to some extent – routinely enter settings where others are going about their business both expecting not to know them, and yet also *expecting to know how they will behave*. And, more than this, we are nearly always absolutely right in both respects. We are only surprised if we encounter someone who is *not* a stranger – 'Fancy meeting you here! Isn't it a small world!'– or if one of these strangers actually does behave strangely – 'Mummy, why is that man shouting?'

Why is this? Why do others do what we expect of them? Why is *dis*order or the *un*expected among strangers so rare?

## STRUCTURAL-CONSENSUS THEORY

One of the traditional ways in which sociologists explain the order and predictability of social life is by regarding human behaviour as *learnt* behaviour. This approach is known – for reasons that will become apparent – as *structural-consensus theory*. The key process this theory emphasises is called *socialisation*. This term refers to the way in which human beings learn the kinds of behaviour expected of them in the social settings in which they find themselves. From this point of view, societies differ because the kinds of behaviour considered appropriate in them differ. People in other societies think and behave differently because they have learned different *rules* about how to behave and think. The same goes for different groups within the same society. The actions and ideas of one group differ from those of another because its members have been socialised into different rules.

Consensus sociologists call the rules which govern thought and behaviour in a society its *culture*. Culture exists prior to the people who learn it. At birth, humans are confronted by a social world already in existence. Joining this world involves learning 'how things are done' in it. Only by learning the cultural rules of a society can a human interact with other humans. Because they have been similarly socialised, different individuals will behave similarly.

Consensus theory thus argues that a society's cultural rules determine, or *structure*, the behaviour of its members, channelling their actions in certain ways rather than others. They do so in much the same way that the physical construction of a building structures the actions of the people inside it. Take the behaviour of students in a school. Once inside the school they will display quite regular patterns of behaviour. They will all walk along corridors, up and down stairs, in and out of classrooms, through doors, and so on. They will, by and large, not attempt to dig through floors, smash through walls, or climb out of windows. Their physical movements are *constrained* by the school building. Since this affects all the students similarly, their behaviour inside the school will be similar – and will exhibit quite definite patterns. In consensus theory, the same is true of social life. Individuals will behave similarly in the same social settings because they are equally constrained by cultural rules. Though these *social structures* are not visible in the way physical structures are, those who are socialised into their rules find them comparably determining.

The levels at which these cultural rules operate can vary. Some rules, like laws for instance, operate at the level of the whole society and structure the behaviour of everyone who lives in it. Others are much less

6

general, structuring the behaviour of people in quite specific social settings. For example, children in a classroom are expected to behave in an orderly and attentive fashion. In the playground much more licence is given them, while away from school their behaviour often bears little resemblance to that expected of them during school hours.

Similarly, when police officers or nurses or members of the armed forces are 'on duty', certain cultural rules structure their behaviour very rigidly. Out of uniform and off duty these constraints do not apply, though other ones do instead – those governing their behaviour as fathers and mothers, or husbands and wives, for instance.

This shows how the theory of a social structure of cultural rules operates. The rules apply not to the individuals themselves, but to the *positions* in the social structure they occupy. Shoppers, police officers, traffic-wardens, schoolteachers or pupils are constrained by the cultural expectations attached to these positions, but only when they occupy them. In other circumstances, in other locations in the social structure – as fathers or mothers, squash players, football supporters, church members, and so on – other rules come into play.

Sociologists call positions in a social structure *roles*. The rules which structure the behaviour of their occupants are called *norms*. There are some cultural rules which are not attached to any particular role or set of roles. Called *values*, these are in a sense summaries of approved ways of living, and act as a base from which particular norms spring. So, for example: 'education should be the key to success'; 'family relationships should be the most important thing to protect'; 'self-help should be the means to individual fulfilment'. All these are values, which provide general principles from which norms directing behaviour in schools and colleges, in the home and at work are derived.

According to this sociological theory, socialisation into norms and values produces agreement, or *consensus*, between people about appropriate behaviour and beliefs, without which no human society can survive. This is why it is called *structural-consensus* theory. Through socialisation, cultural rules structure behaviour, guarantee a consensus about expected behaviour, and thereby ensure social order.

Clearly, in a complex society, there are sometimes going to be competing norms and values. For example, while some people think it is wrong for mothers to go out to work, many women see motherhood at best as a real imposition, and at worst as an infringement of their liberty. Children often encourage each other to misbehave at school and disapprove of their peers who refuse to do so. Teachers usually see this very much the other way round! The Tory Party Conference is annually strident in its condemnation of any speaker who criticises the police. Some young Blacks would be equally furious with any of their number who had *other* than a strongly belligerent attitude towards them.

Consensus theorists explain such differences in behaviour and attitude in terms of the existence of alternative cultural influences, characteristic of different social settings. A good example of this emphasis is their approach to *educational inequality*.

Educational research demonstrates, in the most conclusive fashion, that achievement in education is strongly linked to class membership, gender and ethnic origin. There is overwhelming evidence, for example, that working-class children of similar intelligence to children from middle-class backgrounds achieve far less academically than their middle-class counterparts.

To explain this, consensus theorists turn to stock concepts in their approach to social life – norms, values, socialisation and culture. Starting from the basic assumption that behaviour and belief are caused by socialisation into particular rules, their explanation of working-class underachievement in education seeks to identify:

(a) the cultural influences which propel middle-class children to academic success;
(b) the cultural influences which drag working-class children down to mediocrity.

The argument usually goes something like this. The upbringing of middle-class children involves socialisation into norms and values which are ideal for educational achievement. Because of their own educational experiences, middle-class parents are likely to be very knowledgeable about how education works and how to make the most of it. Further, they are likely to be very keen for their children to make a success of their own education. These children will thus grow up in a social setting where educational achievement is valued, and where they will be constantly encouraged and assisted to fulfil their academic potential.

In contrast, the home background of working-class children often lacks such advantageous socialisation. Working-class parents are likely to have had only limited, and possibly unhappy, experiences of education. Even if they are keen for their children to achieve educational success, they will almost certainly lack the know-how of the middle-class parent to make this happen. Indeed, sometimes they may actively disapprove of academic attainment; for instance, they may simply distrust what they do not know. As a result, their children may well be taught instead to value the more immediate and practical advantages of leaving school as soon as possible. For example, boys may be encouraged to 'learn a trade' – to eschew academic success for the security of an apprenticeship in 'a proper job'. Here is a clear example of the application of consensus theory to the facts of social life.

Different patterns of behaviour are the product of different patterns of socialisation. It might seem that this contradicts the commitment of theorists to the idea that social order in a society is the outcome of an agreement or a consensus among its members about how to behave and what to think. But consensus theorists say that despite differences of culture between different groups, even despite *opposing sub-cultures* within the overall culture, in all societies an *overall* consensus prevails. This is because all societies have certain values about the importance of which there is *no* dispute. They are called either *central values* or *core values*, and socialisation ensures everyone conforms to them.

In Victorian Britain two central values were a commitment to Christian morality, and loyalty to the Queen and the British Empire. Today examples of central values might be the importance of economic growth, the importance of democratic institutions, the importance of the rule of law, and the importance of the freedom of the individual within the law. (Indeed, anything trotted out as 'basic to the British way of life' at any particular time is usually a central value in Britain.)

For consensus theory then, central values are the backbone of social structures, built and sustained by the process of socialisation. Social behaviour and social order are determined by external cultural forces. Social life is possible because of the existence of the social structures of cultural rules.

*Society as a structure of inequality – the influence of advantages and disadvantages on behaviour*

Other sociologists argue a rather different theoretical case from consensus theorists. They agree that society determines our behaviour by structuring or constraining it. But they emphasise different structural constraints. For them, the most important influence on social life is the distribution of advantage, and its impact on behaviour. Where advantages are unequally distributed, the opportunities of the advantaged to choose how to behave are much greater than those of the disadvantaged.

For example, while it is perfectly feasible for two boys of the same intelligence to be equally keen to fulfil their potential in education, and to be equally encouraged by their parents, their culturally instilled enthusiasm cannot, by itself, tell us everything about their potential educational successes or failures. If one boy comes from a wealthy home, while the other is from a much poorer one, this will be far more significant for their education than their similar (learnt) desire. Clearly,

9

the unequal distribution of advantage – in this case material resources – will assist the privileged boy and hamper the disadvantaged one.

The advantaged boy's parents can buy a private education, while those of the poorer boy cannot. The advantaged boy can be assured of living in a substantial enough house, with sufficient space to study, whereas the disadvantaged boy may have to make do with a room with the television in it, or a bedroom shared with his brothers and sisters. The advantaged boy can rely on a proper diet and resulting good health, whereas the disadvantaged boy cannot. The advantaged boy can be guaranteed access to all the books and equipment he needs to study, whereas the disadvantaged boy cannot. Probably most importantly, the advantaged boy will be able to continue his education up to the limit of his potential unhindered. For those who are less advantaged it is often necessary to leave school and go out to work to add to the family income. This stronger impulse usually brings education to a premature end.

## STRUCTURAL-CONFLICT THEORY

One primary objection some sociologists have to structural-consensus theory is that where societies are unequal, people are not *only* constrained by the norms and values they have learnt via socialisation. They are also constrained by the *advantages* they possess – by their position in the *structures of inequality* within their society. This emphasis on the effects on behaviour of an unequal distribution of advantage in a society is usually associated with *structural-conflict* theory. Why are such theories called *conflict* theories?

The kinds of inequality structures in a society vary. Ethnic groups can be unequal, young and old can be unequal, men and women can be unequal, people doing different jobs can be unequal, people of different religious beliefs can be unequal, and so on. The kinds of advantages unequally possessed by such groups can vary, too. Different groups can possess unequal amounts of power, authority, prestige, or wealth, or a combination of these and other advantages.

Notwithstanding the kinds of inequality that conflict theories focus on, and the kinds of advantages they see as unequally distributed, such theories have in common the axiom that the origin and persistence of a structure of inequality lies in the domination of its disadvantaged groups by its advantaged ones. Conflict theories are so-called because for them, a *conflict of interests* between its 'haves' and its 'have-nots' is inherent in an unequal society. As Wes Sharrock (1977) puts it:

The conflict view is . . . founded upon the assumption that . . . any society . . . may provide extraordinarily good lives for some but this is usually only possible because the great majority are oppressed and degraded . . . Differences of *interest* are therefore as important to society as agreements upon rules and values, and most societies are so organised that they not only provide greater benefits for some than for others but in such a way that the accrual of benefits to a few causes positive discomfort to others.

So conflict theory differs from consensus theory not only because it is interested in the way an unequal distribution of advantage in a society structures behaviour, but also because it is interested in the conflict, not the consensus, inherent in such a society. According to conflict theory, there is a conflict of interest between a society's advantaged and disadvantaged, which is inherent in their relationship.

There is another conflict theory objection to consensus theory. Conflict theorists not only accuse consensus theorists of putting too much emphasis on norms and values as determinants of behaviour at the expense of other influences. They also argue that consensus theory misunderstands the role of its key concern – socialisation into culture. Consensus theory argues that people behave as they do because they have been socialised into cultural rules. The outcome is a consensus about how to think and behave, which manifests itself in patterns and regularities of behaviour. Conflict theorists argue that we should see the role of cultural rules and the process of socialisation in a very different light. The real structural determinants of behaviour are the rewards and advantages possessed unequally by different groups in a society. Other things being equal, those most disadvantaged would not put up with such a state of affairs.

Normally, however, other things are *not* equal. Where a society is unequal, the only way it can survive is if those who are disadvantaged in it come to accept their deprivation. Sometimes this involves naked coercion. Plenty of unequal societies survive because their rulers maintain repressive regimes based on terror. The exercise of the force necessary to maintain unequal advantage need not take such an obvious or naked form. Structures of inequality can also survive – and with a surer future – if those most disadvantaged by them can somehow be prevented from seeing themselves as underprivileged. Or, if they do recognise it, if they can be persuaded that this is fair enough – rightful, legitimate and just. The way this happens is through the control and manipulation of the norms and values – the cultural rules – into which people are socialised.

In effect then, for conflict theorists, socialisation is more likely to be an instrument producing social order by means of force and domination, rather than the means to social order via consensus.

Imagine the following scenario. It is early morning in a Latin American country. A group of agricultural labourers, both men and women, are waiting by a roadside for a bus to arrive to drive them to work. Suddenly two vans draw up and four hooded men jump out. At gunpoint they order the labourers into the backs of the vans, which then race away deep into the surrounding countryside. At nightfall they are abandoned and the labourers transferred into a large covered lorry. This is driven through the night, deep into the mountains. Before daybreak it reaches its destination – a huge underground mine, built deep into the heart of a mountain. Here the labourers are horrified to find a vast army of slaves toiling away, under constant surveillance by brutal guards. After being given a meagre meal, the labourers are forced to join this workforce.

As they live out their desperate lives within this mountain world, some of the slaves try to escape. When caught they are publicly punished as a deterrent to others. Two attempts to escape result in public execution. As the labourers get older, they rely on each other for companionship, and on their memories for comfort. They keep sane by recounting stories of their former lives. In the fullness of time, children are born to them. The parents are careful to tell these children all about their past. As the children grow up and have children of *their* own, they, too, are told tales of their grandparents' land of lost content. But for them these are handed-down, historical stories, not tales based on experience. As the years go by, though the facts of life within the mountain remain the same, the perception of life in it by the participants alters. By the time five or six generations of slaves have been born, their knowledge of the world of their ancestors' past lives has become considerably diminished. It is still talked about, sometimes. But by now it is a misted world of folklore and myth. All they know from experience is slavery. So far as any of them can remember, they have always been slaves. In their world, slavery is *'normal'*. In effect, to be a slave means something very different to them from what it meant to their ancestors.

A similar process occurs with the oppressors. As the slaves' view of them has altered over time, so the necessity for naked force has become less and less. As, through socialisation, their subordinates have begun to acquiesce in their own subordination, the guards no longer brandish guns and clubs. Because of this, they no longer see themselves as the original guards did. Both the dominant and the subordinate, knowing nothing else, have, through socialisation, come to see the inequality in their world in a very different light from the original inhabitants.

Though this story is rather larger-than-life, it does allow us to see the role of socialisation into cultural rules as conflict theorists see it. Their argument is that we must be careful not to dismiss the presence of conflict in societies just because a consensus seems to prevail. Naked force is only necessary so long as people see themselves as oppressed. If they can be persuaded that they are not oppressed, or if they fail to see that they are, then they can be willing architects in the design of their own subordination. The easiest way to exercise power, and gain advantage as a result, is for the dominated to be unaware of their subordination.

Rather than simply *describe* cultural rules in a society, therefore, we must carefully examine their content. We must ask: 'Who *benefits* from the *particular* set of rules prevailing in this society, rather than some other set?' Cultural rules cannot be neutral or all-benevolent. Of course people are socialised into pre-existing norms and values. But this tells us only half the story. We must also find out whether some groups *benefit more than others* from the existence of a particular set of rules and have a greater say in their construction and interpretation. If they do, then the process of socialisation into these is an instrument of their advantage.

For example, even a cursory glance at the kinds of occupations held by women and the kinds of rewards they receive for doing them clearly indicates the advantages men have over women in our society. A female prime minister, the occasional female civil servant or MP or judge or university vice-chancellor cannot hide the fact that there is unequal occupational opportunity, and unequal economic reward, based on gender. The facts are that males dominate the best rewarded and most prestigious occupations and (despite the Equal Opportunities Commission) usually receive greater rewards when they perform the same jobs as women.

Clearly, there is a considerable potential conflict of interests between men and women here. It is in men's interests for women not to compete in large numbers for the limited number of highly rewarded jobs. It is in men's interests for women to stay at home and provide domestic services for them. If women were to want something different, this would conflict with the desires, interests and ambitions of men.

So why is it that so many women do *not* object to this state of affairs? If women are as systematically deprived of occupational opportunities and rewards by men as this, why do so many of them acquiesce in their deprivation? For example, why are some of the fiercest critics of the feminist movement women? Why do so many women *choose* to be (unpaid) houseworkers for the benefit of their husbands and children? Why do so many girls *choose* domestic science, needlework and art at school in preference to, say, chemistry, physics or maths? Why is the extent of so many girls' ambitions to 'start a family'? Why do they not wish to explore their potential in other activities instead, or as well?

Clearly, a substantial part of the answers to these questions is that women have been socialised into accepting this definition of themselves. For conflict theorists this is a clear example of particular norms and values working in the interests of one section of society and against another. Through the ideas they have learnt, women have been forced to accept a role which is subordinate to men.

There is one final question to be asked about this theoretical approach. How does the exercise of force by means of socialisation into particular ideas happen? Conflict theorists say it can be intentional or unintentional. The rulers of many societies in the world today deliberately employ *propaganda* to persuade the ruled of the legitimacy of this arrangement. They also often control and *censor* mass media in their countries, to ensure lack of opposition to this controlled socialisation.

The exercise of this kind of force can be less deliberate too. Take our example of the inequality between men and women in our society. To what extent does the image of women presented in advertising promote an acceptance of this inequality? Though the intention is to sell various products – from lingerie and perfume to household goods, to alcohol, cigarettes, cars and office equipment – the images of women used in advertising are so specific that there are other, less intentional effects, too. Two images dominate. One is of the woman as the domestic at home, using the 'best' products to clean, polish, launder and cook. The other is of the woman as a sexually desirable object, guaranteed to either (i) magically adorn the life of any male who is sensible enough to drink a certain sort of gin, drive a particular car or use a specific shaving lotion; or (ii) be transformed into an irresistible seductress when she wears particular underwear or perfume, or is given a particular brand of chocolates.

Such advertising socialises both men *and* women, of course. The outcome is a stereotypical view of womanhood and of the place of women in society, embraced not only by those whom it disadvantages, but also by those who benefit from it. There *is* a consensus about such things. However, it is not the kind of consensus portrayed by the consensus theorist. It is an *imposed* consensus, preventing the conflict that would break out if people were allowed to see the world as it *really* is.

There are a number of sociological theories that can be called structural-conflict theories, in that they are based on two main premises: (1) social structures consist of unequally advantaged groups. The interests of these groups are in conflict, since inequality results from

14

the domination and exploitation of disadvantaged groups by advantaged ones.

(2) social order in such societies is maintained by force – either by actual force, or by force exercised through socialisation.

Structural-consensus theory and structural-conflict theory thus emphasise different kinds of influences on thought and behaviour. Though both theories see the origin of human social life in the influences or determinants of society external to the individual, they disagree about what this outside society consists of. Consensus theory is based on the primacy of the influence of culture – what we learn to want as a result of socialisation. Conflict theory, in contrast, pays most attention to the conflict inherent in the relationship between unequally advantaged groups in society and argues that the content of culture should be seen as a means of perpetuating relationships of inequality.

*Society as the creation of its members – the influence of interpretation on behaviour*

A third kind of sociological theory leads in a rather different direction. It still attempts to explain why human beings in society behave in the orderly ways they do. But instead of looking for the answer in the influence of a social structure which people confront and are constrained by, this theory argues something else. From this point of view, the most important influence on an individual's behaviour is the behaviour of other individuals towards him or her. The focus is not on general cultural rules, or on the unequal distribution of advantage in whole societies. It is on the way individual pieces of social interaction proceed; on how the parties to them are able to understand one another. This is not to say that structural theories do not try to explain this, too. In consensus theory, for example, people are role players, and act out parts learnt through socialisation. But how do they decide *which* roles to play, in *which* social setting? Consensus theory does not try to explain why people choose one role rather than another. It is assumed that we somehow learn to make the right choices. This third theory, however, argues that the choice of role playing is much more complex than in this rather robotised view. It argues that the *essence* of social life lies in the quite extraordinary ability of humans to *work out what is going on around them*, and then *to choose to act in a particular way, in the light of this interpretation*. This is called *interpretive*, or *action theory*.

## ACTION THEORY

Action theorists stress the need to concentrate on the micro-level of social life – the way particular individuals are able to interact with one another – rather than on the *macro*-level – the way the whole structure of society influences the behaviour of individuals. They argue that we must not think societies exist outside of, and prior to, the interaction of individuals. For action theorists, societies are the end result of human interaction, not its cause. Only by looking at how individual humans are able to interact can we come to understand how social order is created. To see how this happens, let us reflect on the kinds of action of which humans are capable.

Some human action is like the action of phenomena in the inanimate world – purposeless, or lacking intention. We all do things involuntarily – like sneezing, blinking or yawning. We do not *choose* to feel fear, excitement, or pain, or choose to react in certain ways to those feelings. So far as we know, the actions of non-human *animate* phenomena are purely instinctive (automatic or reflex responses to external stimuli). It is true that animals, for example, often appear to act in a purposive way by using their brains. They seem to choose to eat or sleep or be friendly or aggressive, or to evacuate their bladders over the new living-room carpet. However, the usual zoological explanation is that even these often quite sophisticated patterns of animal action are involuntary. They are reactive and conditioned, rather than the product of voluntary creative decision-making.

Nearly all human action *is* voluntary. It is the product of a conscious decision to act, a result of thought. Nearly everything we do is the result of choosing to act in one way rather than another. Furthermore, this is purposive, or goal-oriented choice. We choose between courses of action because, as humans, we are able to aim at an end or a goal and take action to achieve this. Nearly all human action, therefore, is *intentional* action: we *mean* to do what we do in order to achieve our chosen purposes.

Where do these chosen purposes, or goals, come from? What action theory emphasises is that we decide what to do *in the light of our interpretation of the world around us*. Being human means walking about in the social world, making sense of the settings or situations in which we find ourselves and choosing to act accordingly. To use the usual action theory phrase for this, we choose what to do in the light of our 'definition of the situation'. For example, suppose you wake up one summer morning to find the sun shining in a cloudless sky. You decide

16

to sunbathe all day and to mow your lawn in the evening, when it will be cooler. At lunchtime, you see large clouds beginning to form in the distance. Because you decide there is a chance of a thunderstorm, you cut the grass immediately. You get very hot. It does not rain. In the evening, you go for a walk in the country. You come to a country pub and stop for a drink. As you sit outside you notice smoke rising on a hillside some distance away. As you watch the smoke gets thicker and darker. You decide the fire is unattended and out of control. You dash inside the pub and ring the fire brigade. Shortly afterwards you hear a fire engine racing to the fire. You climb a nearby hill to have a better look. When you get there you see that the fire is, in fact, deliberate; it is a bonfire in the garden of a house on the hillside which you had been unable to see from the pub. Shortly afterwards you hear the fire engine returning to its base. You go back to the pub to finish your drink. It has been cleared away in your absence. You have no more money. You decide it is not your day. You decide to go home.

Of course, nearly all of the settings we have to make sense of involve more than this because nearly everything we do in our lives takes place in the company of others. Most of the situations we have to define in order to choose how to act are *social*; they involve *other* humans doing things. You see a very large man shaking his fist and shouting at you, and conclude that he is not overjoyed that you have driven into the back of his car. As a result you decide not to suggest that he was responsible for the accident because of the way he parked. You see a traffic warden slipping a parking ticket under your windscreen-wiper, and decide not to contribute to the Police Benevolent Fund after all. This is *social* action. It is action we choose to take in the light of what we interpret the behaviour of others to mean.

There is more to social action than interpretation leading to action, however. Most of the time when we interact with other humans, they *want* us to arrive at certain interpretations of their actions – they *want* us to think one thing of them rather than another. The man whose car has just been damaged is not behaving in the rather distinctive manner described above because he wishes the culprit to come round to his house for tea. The man scratching his nose in the auction room is not (usually) alleviating an itch. He is communicating his bid to the auctioneer, and he expects that the latter will interpret his actions as he wishes. Pedestrians in London streets do not wave to taxi-drivers because they are, or want to become, their friends. They do so because they want a lift.

Dress can often organise interpretation just as effectively as gestures, of course. Though the punk rocker, the skinhead, the bowler-hatted civil servant, the police officer and the traffic warden whom we encounter in the street make no *apparent* attempt to communicate with us, they are certainly doing so, nevertheless. They want us to think certain things about them when we see them, so they choose to communicate by the use of uniforms. They are making a symbolic use of dress, if you like; after all, like gestures, garments symbolise what their users want us to interpret about them.

The most effective symbols humans have at their disposal are words – *linguistic* symbols. Though dress, gesture, touch and even smell can often communicate our meanings and organise the interpretations of others adequately enough, clearly the most efficient – and most remarkable – way in which we can get others to understand us is through language. This is why action theorists are often interested in the way we use language to exchange meanings with each other. Language, verbal or written, is the uniquely human device which we are able to use to interact meaningfully with one another, and thereby to create society.

From this point of view, societies are made up of individuals engaging in a countless number of meaningful encounters. The result is social order. But this is no *determined* order. It is not the result of the imposition of cultural rules, as the consensus theorist sees it. Nor is it the result of the constraints of a world where advantages are unequally distributed, and where cultural rules legitimate these constraints, as the conflict theorist sees it. Instead, society is an order created, or accomplished, by the capacities of the members themselves. It is the result of numerous occasions of interaction, carried out by interpreting, meaning-attributing actors who can make sense of the social settings in which they find themselves and who choose courses of action accordingly.

There is another important difference between structural and interpretive conceptions of society. For structural theorists, the character of a society – its social structure – is not in doubt. It is a 'real' thing which exists outside of its members. For the interpretivist, however, it is much more difficult to describe a society which is the outcome of interpretation as somehow 'true' or 'real'.

For the interpretivist, being human involves interpreting what is going on around one – saying: 'This is what is happening here', and choosing an appropriate course of action in the light of this interpretation. Such interpretations of 'what is going on here' can only ever be considered 'correct' or 'true' for the particular person doing the interpreting. What is 'really' going on depends on the individual.

Reality is indeed in the eye of the beholder. We act in ways we consider appropriate. What we consider appropriate depends upon what we think the behaviour of others means. It is therefore by no means inconceivable that other people, in exactly the same social situations as ourselves, will take the behaviour around them to mean something very different, and will therefore take very different courses of action from us. For example, a car crashes into a wall on a wet winter's evening. The police officer called to the scene discovers a dead driver and a strong smell of drink in the car. A search reveals an empty whisky bottle underneath a seat. Like all humans encountering a social situation, the officer engages in a process of interpretation, defining the situation. Weighing up the evidence, he or she decides that the crash was an accident caused by the driver being drunk and losing control of the vehicle in difficult driving conditions. *Another* officer called to the scene might use this evidence to interpret things rather differently, however. He or she might consider the possibility that the driver deliberately drove the car into the wall as an act of suicide, having first given himself courage to do so by drinking the whisky. The second officer would then make inquiries that the first would not. The dead man's domestic and work affairs would be looked into and it might be discovered that he recently separated from his wife, losing custody of his children. The officer would decide that his suspicions of suicide had been sufficiently confirmed by this additional evidence, and that it should be given at the Coroner's court when the inquest was held.

How the death is finally interpreted depends upon the decision of the court, of course, when the evidence is reassessed by a new set of interpreters – particularly the Coroner. The Coroner's decision will define the death as either accidental or a suicide. Is the judgment the 'truth'? Who is to say what was the 'reality' of the situation? What 'really' happened here? In the case of this kind of example, of course, no one will ever know.

Even in more conclusive circumstances, actions still always depend upon the interpretation of the beholder. Suppose you come across a middle-aged man grappling with a young girl in the bushes of a park. What you do depends on what you think is going on. You may decide the man is assaulting the girl, and take a course of action you see fit in the light of this interpretation (and depending how brave you feel at the time). Or you may decide it is horseplay between lovers, or a father admonishing his daughter – or any other interpretation that may spring to mind. What matters is not so much that you are *right*, that you see what is *really* happening, but that:

(a) you *cannot help* but come to some sort of interpretation or other (even if it is that you do *not* know what is happening) and;

(b) what you decide to do will be the result of this interpretation.

Though subsequent events may 'prove' things one way or another, initial action undertaken by human beings in such social circumstances, though always involving a process of interpretation, can never be assumed to be definitely 'true' or 'real'. It can only ever be how we choose to see things. The world 'is' what we think it is. As W. I. Thomas (1966) puts it: 'If man defines situations as real, they are real in their consequences'. In contrast to the structuralist view then, social 'reality' is not a factual, objective, unambiguous state of affairs. Reality can only ever be what the actors involved in interaction *think* is real, since what they *think* is real determines what they decide to do. Reality is therefore quite definitely the negotiated creation of individuals in interaction with one another. Furthermore, because the social worlds so created are dependent on the interpretations of particular individuals in particular social settings, they are much more precarious constructions than suggested by the notion of social structures determining behaviour.

Consensus, conflict and action theories thus identify different factors as significant in explaining the nature of social life, and of the relationship between the individual and society. Shortly we will look in detail at the work of some significant sociologists of the nineteenth and twentieth centuries. As we shall see, for most of the time sociology has been in existence as a distinct discipline, the kinds of issues highlighted by consensus, conflict and action approaches have been central to sociological theorising. Although only some of this theorising falls neatly or exclusively within one of these traditions alone, they are nonetheless useful as reference points from which to understand differences and debates in sociological thought.

The work of three nineteenth century sociologists in particular has reverberated through the twentieth century and it is for this reason that they are regarded as the classic figures in the discipline. They are a Frenchman, Emile Durkheim (1858–1917) and two Germans, Karl Marx (1818–1883) and Max Weber (1864–1920). Despite the great differences in the content and direction of their sociological theories, the work of Durkheim, Marx and Weber each represents an intellectual and political response to the same historical circumstances. The most powerful set of forces at work in nineteenth-century Europe was unleashed in the seventeenth and eighteenth centuries during the period historians call the Enlightenment; today these forces are summarised in sociology as *modernity*. Sociology came into being because of modernity, and the theories of many of its major figures in both the nineteenth and twentieth centuries can be seen as different kinds of responses to the rise

KEIGHLEY COLLEGE LIBRARY

of the modern world. This is particularly true of the classic writings of Durkheim, Marx and Weber.


## MODERNITY AND MODERNISM


The idea of the 'modern' originated as an account of the kinds of ideas and behaviour that grew out of the decline of medieval society in Europe. The three elements in modernity – economic, political and cultural – have been summarised as follows:

> *Economically*, modernity involved the capitalistic practices of a market economy. It involved the growth of production for profit, wage labour as the principal form of employment, the development of industrial technology, and the extension of the division of labour. *Politically*, modernity involved the consolidation of the centralised nation state and the extension of bureaucratic forms of administration, systematic forms of surveillance, and democratic political party systems. *Culturally*, modernity involved a challenge to 'tradition' in the name of 'rationality' and a stress on the virtues of scientific and technical knowledge. (*Social Studies Review*, September 1990.)

It is this cultural change in belief about what constitutes knowledge and what knowledge is for, that directly promoted the rise of sociology and sociological theorising. Modernist thinking involves the idea that the purpose of acquiring knowledge is, as Tony Giddens (1987) puts it: 'To influence for the better the human condition.' For modernity implies the constant pursuit of improvement in human lives and of the pursuit of *progress*. Unlike traditional settings, where virtue lies in things remaining the same, in modern worlds change, development and improvement are the goals; as Cheal (1991) has pointed out, believing in the ideal and possibility of progress means 'believing that things tomorrow can always be better than they are today, which in turn means being prepared to overturn the existing order of things in order to make way for progress. It means, in other words, being prepared to break with tradition'.

How should this progress be achieved? Underpinning the belief in the possibility of progress is a belief in the power of reason – in the ability of humans to think about themselves, their condition and their society *reflexively* and *rationally* – and to improve it in the light of such rational

21

thought. The idea that humans can not only think about, and explain, their lives – to produce *social theories* in fact – but can employ them to change society for the better, is a specifically modern notion. The idea that *reason* can provide an agenda and a set of prescriptions for living, rather than relying on divine intervention and instruction, only began to prevail after the Enlightenment. Summarising the effects of the Enlightenment, Badham (1986) says:

> It was during this period that faith in divine revelation, and the authority of the Church as interpreter of God's will, were increasingly undermined by this new confidence in the ability of human reason to provide an understanding of the world and a guide for human conduct. Similarly, the understanding of history as the chronicle of the fall of man from God's grace, with spiritual salvation only attainable in the next world, was largely replaced by a belief in human perfectibility and the increasing faith in man's power and ability to use his new-found knowledge to improve mankind's state. The importance of these two assumptions should not be underestimated. Without the faith in reason, social theory could not be regarded as playing any important role in society. Without the belief in the possibility of progress, whatever reason's ability to understand the nature of society, social theory would not be able to fulfil any positive role in improving upon man's fate.

So sociology is a product of modernity – of a belief in the power of human reason to create knowledge, which can be used to achieve progress – and its subject matter is the world created by modernity: Giddens (1987) has said that in sociology, the 'prime field of study is the social world brought about by the advent of modernity'. As Giddens (1987) also puts it, the very existence of sociology is 'bound up with the "project of modernity" '. The construction of social theories thus reflects a concern not only with *how* we live, but how we *should* live; social theories of modern society try not only to describe and explain our social world, but to diagnose its problems and propose solutions. According to Giddens (1987), this places sociology in the 'tensed zone of transition between diagnosis and prognosis'.

The problem, of course, concerns the goal and direction of desirable change. The reason for the existence of sociological *theories* rather than for a sociological *theory*, is, according to Bilton *et al.* (1987) that while 'most great sociologists have been inspired by their concern to improve society, they have differed fundamentally in their definitions of the desirable relationship between humans and their society' – that is, of how to do it. The following chapters attempt to summarise the contributions of some influential nineteenth- and twentieth-century sociological figures to this enterprise – the contribution of sociology to the 'project of modernity'.

# CHAPTER TWO

# *Durkheim and functionalism*

Functionalism is inextricably bound up with the work of its first major exponent, the Frenchman Emile Durkheim (1858–1917). Other significant functionalists have been leading British social anthropologists in the years between 1920 and 1960. Of particular importance has been the work of anthropology's first two major figures, Bronislaw Malinowski and A. R. Radcliffe-Brown. In addition, the later writings of anthropologists like E. E. Evans-Pritchard, Meyer Fortes and Max Gluckman all helped to establish functionalist theory in British social science.

In twentieth-century sociology, undoubtedly the major figure (from the 1930s to the late 1950s) has been the American functionalist Talcott Parsons, though other US functionalists like R. K. Merton and Kingsley Davis have been important too. Until the 1960s America dominated sociology, and social anthropology dominated British social science. So, from the years between the early 1920s and the late 1950s, though other theoretical perspectives had long been in existence, they had little impact. The theoretical stage was dominated by the functionalist version of structural-consensus theory.

Though it has since lost much of its influence in sociological theory, particularly outside the US, an understanding of contemporary theoretical alternatives in sociology must begin with an understanding of functionalism. In a very real sense, the rise to prominence of conflict theories (mainly in the forms of Marxist theory and in some versions of feminist theory) and action theories (like Weberian theory, symbolic-interactionism and ethnomethodology) as major sociological approaches can only be understood in the light of the criticisms that began to be made (and by the late 1950s, very loudly) of functionalism. Conflict theories and action theory did not come into being in opposition to functionalism. However, they rose to prominence when they did because for many sociologists they provided questions and answers about social life which functionalism could not. Let us see why.

## EMILE DURKHEIM

Durkheim's response to modernism has two main elements:
(1) he wanted to ensure that harmonious orderly societies could be created;
(2) he wanted to create a *science* of society to generate the knowledge necessary to show how this could be done.

Durkheim had a quite orthodox consensus view of social structures. Their crucial feature, he said, is that they are made up of *norms* and *values* – cultural definitions of behaviour considered appropriate and worthy in different settings. Since it is through socialisation that we learn these normative definitions, it is only this process which makes individuals members of society and, therefore, makes social life possible.

According to Durkheim, though we may think we choose to behave in one way rather than another, in reality the choice is made for us. It was Durkheim who first of all stressed the consensus view that (as Lucy Mair, 1972, put it) 'even the possibilities of thought and experience are *inherited*, not invented'. For example, people who attend a religious service may believe in their god sincerely. But the beliefs and practices of their religion were in existence before they were – they *learnt* them. Like all other social activity, religious belief and practice is structured by society, and by the positions of people in it. Durkheim himself (1938) makes this point, so fundamental to the consensus view of social life:

> When I fulfil my obligations as brother, husband, or citizen I perform duties which are defined, externally to myself and my acts, in law and custom. Even if they conform to my own sentiments, and I feel their reality subjectively, such reality is still objective, for I did not create them; I merely inherited them through my education . . . the church member finds the beliefs and practices of his religious life ready made at birth; their existence prior to him implies their existence outside himself.

For Durkheim, then, the achievement of social life among humans, and the existence of social order in society – which he calls 'social solidarity' – is ensured by culture: collective standards or rules of behaviour. (Durkheim's phrase for these rules was 'social facts'.) Although these are only *visible* through the conformity of individuals to them, they are, nevertheless, in Durkheim's words, 'external to, and constraining upon' these individuals. Though not capable of being seen, such structures of cultural rules are as real to the individuals whose behaviour is determined by them as the world's physical structure which they also

25

confront. Society, in a famous phrase of Durkheim's, is a reality *'sui generis'* – it has its own existence.

It is this conception of his subject matter that leads Durkheim to advocate the use of science to explain social life. The scientific method he favoured is known as *positivism*.

The guiding principle for the positivist scientist is that if something exists in nature, it has been caused by something else in nature. That is, natural phenomena cause other natural phenomena. For example, when water reaches a certain temperature (cause) it freezes (effect). Furthermore, this always happens. There are no circumstances (depending on atmospheric pressure) when water will not become ice at a particular temperature. Such invariable cause and effect relationships are called *laws*. Science sets out to discover the laws of nature. These laws are 'given' for us. Whether we like it or not, water *will* freeze at a certain temperature. Whether we like it or not, the temperature *is* higher in the summer than in the winter. Whether we like it or not, leaves *will* fall from deciduous trees in the autumn. We live in a natural world that is organised in a particular way and we are stuck with this world, whatever our views about it. Science therefore only reveals *why* nature is as it is. We can describe this 'given' character of nature by saying it is an *objective* world. It exists, as a matter of fact, independently of any *subjective* feelings or judgements we may have about it.

For Durkheim, social structures are as objective and given as nature. For him, social structures are as given for the inhabitants of a society who encounter them at birth as is the natural world given for phenomena, animate and inanimate, that make *it* up. Daffodils do not choose to be yellow; frogs do not choose to croak and have bulging eyes; water does not choose to freeze. They do so, nevertheless. Humans do not choose to have two eyes, a nose and a mouth. Nor do they choose to have two arms and two legs. These are simply biological facts of life.

In the same way, for Durkheim, a society consists of a similar realm of *social* facts – 'external to and constraining upon' the individual. We do not choose to believe the things we believe or to act in the way we act. We *learn* to think or do these things. Pre-existing cultural rules *determine* our ideas and behaviour through socialisation. Thus, in the same way as the characteristics of natural phenomena are the product of laws of nature, so people's ideas and acts are the product of external social forces that make up social structures. As Durkheim (1938) said: 'The laws of societies are no different from those governing the rest of nature and the method by which they are discovered is identical with that of the other sciences'.

For positivist science this method involves *empirical observation*: only if you can muster evidence of causal relationships identifiable by the senses can you claim to have *demonstrated* their existence. Thus, Durkheim argues for sociology to rely on empirical evidence too. Since behaviour and belief are determined by external structural forces, when we quantify the incidence of action, or of thought among people, what we have is empirical evidence of the extent to which the forces that have produced this behaviour and belief exist.

The attraction of this method of relying on empirical evidence to produce knowledge was that it seemed to offer the possibility of certainty – of demonstrable proof. For many of those engaged in a project dedicated to social reconstruction and societal progress – the sociology of the modern world – such a prospect was indeed enticing. Durkheim's French predecessor, Auguste Comte (1798–1857), was the first to proclaim the virtues of an empirically-based social science. According to Bilton *et al.* (1987) for someone like Comte, born during the aftermath of the French Revolution, the implications of such a social science were enormous: 'for positive sociological knowledge could offer the means for peaceful reconstruction of social order by the elite of enlightened scientists and intellectuals – social change need not depend upon revolutionary violence and the manipulation of the mob'.

Durkheim inherited this tradition and built upon it. He saw as his mission the establishment of a science of society which could prescribe how societies could be organised, in the light of knowledge of the laws governing social behaviour, in an ordered fashion.

According to Durkheim, then, order flows from consensus – from the existence of shared norms and values. For him, the key cause of social and individual ill-health stems from *anomie* – a lack of regulating norms. Anomie is the result of the potential scourge of modern competitive society – the promotion of unrestricted desires; without norms constraining behaviour, 'humans develop insatiable appetites, limitless desires and general feelings of irritation and dissatisfaction'. Durkheim (1974) went on to say that a strong, ordered society and individual liberation are only guaranteed where beliefs and behaviour are properly regulated by socialisation: 'The individual submits to society and this submission is the condition of his liberation. For man freedom consists in the deliverance from blind, unthinking physical forces; this he achieves by opposing against them the great and intelligent force which is society, under whose protection he shelters'.

Why is order, harmony, and consensus the right state of affairs?

## THE ORGANISMIC ANALOGY

Durkheim used the work of an Englishman, Herbert Spencer, to argue that we can best understand the existence and character of social structures by comparing them to the origins and workings of biological organisms. As the name suggests, an organism is a living entity whose existence and health depend on all the organs that make it up working properly together. In the human body, for instance, all the organs are *interdependent*. The workings of the brain depend on the workings of the lungs, which depend on the workings of the heart, and so on. Furthermore, all (or nearly all, in the case of the human body) of these organs are *indispensable*. Each exists because it satisfies a particular need of the human body, which no other organ can. For example, the heart exists because of the need for an organ to pump blood round the body, the liver exists because of the need for the blood to be purified, the kidneys exist because of the need to dispose of waste matter and so on. In other words, the reason why each of the constituent parts of the body exists is because each performs a particular *function* for the overall system. Furthermore, all these necessary parts have to function together in an *integrated* way for the system as a whole to work properly. The difference between referring to integrated wholes as 'systems' rather than 'structures' can be understood as simply the difference between a static picture of the whole – its structure – and what this looks like when it is actually working – as a system. In sociology the terms are often used in association with each other for just this reason. A society both has a structure and works as a system.

Durkheim argues that a social system works like an organic system. Societies are made up of structures of cultural rules – established beliefs and practices – to which their members are expected to conform. Sociologists describe any established way of thinking or acting in a society into which its members are socialised as being *institutionalised* in that society. For functionalists, the institutions of a society – for example the kind of family form it has, its political arrangements, its educational arrangements, its religious arrangements, and so on – are analogous to the parts of an organism. Societies consist of parts which are integrated and interdependent. As with organs, the reason why an institutionalised way of thinking or acting exists in a society is that it plays an indispensable part – or, to use the functionalist phrase – *performs a necessary function* – in maintaining the society in a stable and satisfactory state. In the case of the human body, if any organ fails to perform properly, ill-health, or even loss of life, is the result. For Durkheim, such a functional failure by an institution – if it malfunctions – also leads to a comparable state for the whole social system. Functionalists have various phrases to describe this; a 'loss of social solidarity', a 'lack of integration', or a 'loss of equilibrium' are three favourite ones.

Crucially, therefore, this account of the origins and workings of societies means that the existence of a social institution, of a part of the social structure, is not the result of *the members of a society deciding* to act or think this way. After all, people do not *decide* to have bowels, or a liver or a pair of kidneys. These organs exist because the body needs them to perform necessary functions. In the same way, in functionalist theory, the institutional arrangements of a society exist not because of any choice on the part of its members. They are there because they are performing a necessary function for the social structure as a whole. Durkheim and other functionalists therefore argue that we should always explain the existence of social arrangements by looking for the *function* being performed by them – for the needs of the social system as a whole that they are satisfying.

The use of this analogy makes clear the goals of the theory. The purpose is to specify the importance of seeing the good society as the integrated, stable society. Organisms do not remain healthy if the constituent organs fight, eat or kill each other. There is a unity of purpose in organisms – the pursuit, protection and retention of health. So it is with social systems.

Therefore, the role of sociology should be the use of science to reveal the laws governing social organisation. These laws demonstrate that the function of institutions is to serve the needs of the social system. 'Institutions performing functions', or 'institutions serving the needs of the social system' is functionalist jargon for people living their lives in the right ways – from which society benefits. So, 'ensuring that institutions perform these functions', means people knowing, and agreeing, about how to behave; thus, socialisation into the correct rules is the key. The end result is a world where everyone agrees about how life should be lived, institutions perform their functions, the needs of the social system are satisfied and the society is healthy.

The corollary of this is that if the society is *un*healthy – you can tell because it will be disordered, riven with conflict, division and disagreement – it is because socialisation is deficient. In these circumstances political action is necessary in the light of the social scientific evidence to ensure the correct cultural prescriptions are re-established. The end result is a harmonious society – integrated, stable, cohesive and healthy – and happy, normatively-guided individuals.

How does science reveal the correct ways of living – the laws governing social organisation? It demonstrates, empirically, the benefits for the social system of correctly functioning institutions.

## DURKHEIM'S FUNCTIONAL THEORY OF RELIGION

The following is a simple example of the application of functionalist theory taken from one of Durkheim's own works, called *The Elementary Forms of Religious Life* (1976).

There is an aborigine people called the Arunta, who live in Australia. They are divided up into two kinds of group. *Bands* are their domestic groups who live together day to day, eking out a meagre survival by hunting and gathering in the bush. The Arunta also belong to much larger groups, called *clans*. Much like the Scottish clans of great importance long ago, each Arunta clan consists of people who believe themselves to be descended from a distant common ancestor – that is, they consider themselves to be related. Each clan has a *totem* – an object in natural life which Arunta clan members believe to be special to them. In fact, the totem is so special that, according to Durkheim, they imbue it with a religious significance. On rare but important occasions the whole of the clan (including members of many different bands, of course) gathers to worship the totem. In addition, during their day-to-day life as band members, whenever they come across their particular totem they treat it with reverence – as a kind of *sacred* object.

How should we explain this? Employing the assumptions of functionalist theory, Durkheim is not interested in any intentions of particular Arunta individuals to have totemism in their society. After all, it was present among them before they were born, and will continue to be there after they die. He wants instead to identify the *function* that totemism performs for the Arunta social system. The answer he gives is this.

Living such a precarious life (without things we take for granted like hospitals or welfare institutions), the Arunta people above all need *each other* to survive. The groups to which the Arunta belong are their lifeline; the obligations others feel to help them, when they need it, are their only hope. In these circumstances, argues Durkheim, what is needed is some means of ensuring that the group *remains* important in the eyes of Arunta individuals. Furthermore, the recognition of the obligations must extend beyond band members alone. If not, all that would happen (as it does so often between people who feel no obligation towards one another) would be that individual bands would compete, and fight for, the limited resources available in their world. They would soon wipe each other out.

In the Arunta social system the answer to this problem of need for integration of separate groups is *totemism*. The totem is, as Durkheim puts it, 'the flag of the clan'. It is a *symbol* of those people in Arunta society with whom band members do not live, but whom they look upon as relatives. They are special people who should be helped and supported whenever necessary. Because of the totem, the group's symbol, its members are reminded of the group's existence when they might otherwise forget it. On the ceremonial occasions when the whole group gathers to worship the totem, a collective reaffirmation of its importance to them takes place. As Durkheim puts it, by worshipping the totem, the Arunta are really worshipping the group.

The *function* of totemism, then, is to *integrate* the Arunta social system (to draw its parts together and sustain it as a whole). It is, in Durkheim's terms, an instrument of *social solidarity*. Clearly, totemism is here being explained not in terms of what it *is* – what the content of its doctrines or beliefs are – but what it *does*, that is, the function it performs for the social system. Functionalists since Durkheim have extended this analysis to all religions. For them, religion must always exist, since all social systems need integrating. They argue that what is interesting is not what is *different* about the beliefs and rituals characteristic of, say, totemism, Buddhism, Hinduism, Judaism, Protestantism and Catholicism. For them, what is interesting is what is *similar* about what they each *do* – about the *integrative functions* all these religions perform for their social sytems.

In recent times, of course, functionalists have been faced with the rather tricky problem of explaining how religion, which they saw as essential for the continuance of society, could have become so unimportant in so many of them. Undeterred, some have argued that even though religion has apparently lost importance in many societies (a process known as *secularisation*), the function of integration continues to be performed by present-day functional equivalents of religion. Some theorists have claimed that this happens even in anti-religious societies, such as some (now-defunct) communist countries of Eastern Europe. Commitment to communist ideas, and the holding of rituals, like the May Day parades in the former Soviet Union, were said to be equivalent to religion. They were said to meet the need for a shared set of values and collective rituals met by more orthodox religious beliefs and practices in other societies.

Even in highly secularised Western societies some functionalists have seen a new kind of religion performing ancient functions. Robert Bellah argues for the existence of a 'civil religion' in the USA, in which American history and institutions are utilised to ensure the reaffirmation of essential American values and sentiments. As Roy Wallis (1983) puts it:

> Bellah finds evidence for the existence of civil religion in such events as Presidential Inaugurations. Inaugural addresses tend to be

couched in a religious idiom, referring to God in general terms and to the travails of America as a modern Israel led out of Egypt. This stylised rhetoric is taken as indicating a real commitment on the part of participants to symbols and values which unify and integrate the community and provide sacred legitimation for its affairs. Other more frequent ceremonials such as Thanksgiving Day and Memorial Day are similarly held to integrate families into the civil religion, or to unify the community around its values.

What is very apparent here is an interest in the effects of a religion, rather than its constituent beliefs. First, many different kinds of religious belief-systems are lumped together, because of the similar integrative function they all perform. Second, very different kinds of belief-systems, without any reference to, for example, gods or spirits or an afterlife, are nevertheless thought of as equivalent to religion. Again, this is because of the similar function they are seen as performing. This directs our attention to a principal characteristic of functionalist explanation. Clearly, the inhabitants of India, Ireland or Israel would argue that their religions are not similar at all, since their focus would be on the beliefs themselves, not their effects. For the functionalist, however, the explanation of a belief or a pattern of behaviour observable in a society held by the *members* of that society is not usually thought to be particularly relevant. For them, the often unintended consequences of people's actions and beliefs needs to be identified – those consequences which, though not necessarily apparent to the people concerned, nevertheless have a crucial functional effect for the social system. To distinguish between these two levels of analysis, functionalists generally refer to the 'manifest' function of institutions (those of which people are aware) and their 'latent' functions (those of which people are often *un*aware). These latent functions are even more important to identify in order to understand the functioning and persistence of social systems.

These, then, are the characteristic features of functional analysis:
(a) an interest in the *effect* of an activity or belief, rather than its constituent *ingredients*: what it *does*, rather than what it *is*;
(b) a stress on the need to go beyond people's own explanations of their activities in order to reveal the true functional significance of institutionalised behaviour and belief.

By looking at a famous example from functionalist anthropology we will be able to see the character and consequences of these core functionalist interests.

## THE KULA

Bronislaw Malinowski was the first anthropologist to undertake a long-term piece of field research. For four years (between 1915 and 1918), he lived among the Trobriand Islanders, who inhabit a group of tiny coral islands off the coast of New Guinea. He published a number of books describing and explaining various aspects of Trobriand life, but the most famous is *Argonauts of the Western Pacific*. This is an account of an elaborate gift-exchange institution, called the *kula*, which is carried on by the Trobrianders among themselves and with the members of other tribal societies who live on surrounding islands. Malinowski (1922) described the kula as follows:

The kula is a form of exchange, of extensive, inter-tribal character; it is carried on by communities inhabiting a wide ring of islands which form a closed circuit . . . along this route, articles of the two kinds, and these two kinds only, are constantly travelling in opposite directions. In the directions of the hands of a clock, moves constantly one of these kinds – long necklaces of red shell, called *soulava*. In the opposite direction moves the other kind – bracelets of white shell called *mwali*. Each of these two articles as it travels in its own direction on the closed circuit, meets on its way articles of the other class and is constantly being exchanged for them. Every movement of the kula articles, every detail of the transactions is fixed and regulated by a set of traditional rules and conventions, and some acts of the kula are accompanied by an elaborate magical ritual and public ceremonies.

On every island and in every village, a more or less limited number of men take part in the kula – that is to say, receive the goods, hold them for a short time, and then pass them on. Therefore every man who is in the kula, periodically though not regularly, receives one of several mwali (arm-shells), or a soulava necklace (necklace of red shell disks), and then has to hand it on to one of his partners, from whom he receives the opposite commodity in exchange. Thus no man ever keeps any of the articles for any length of time in his possession. One transaction does not finish the kula relationship, the rule being 'once in the kula, always in the kula', and a partnership between two men is a permanent and life-long affair. Again, any given mwali or soulava may always be found travelling and changing hands, and there is no question of its ever settling down, so that the principle 'once in the kula, always in the kula' applies also to the valuables themselves.

33

How is such an institution to be explained? Malinowski argues that from the point of view of those involved in it, the kula is a significant way of gaining prestige. In industrial society, objects are used in order to gain prestige too, of course. Thorstein Veblen coined the famous phrase 'conspicuous consumption' to describe the way people in Western societies do not simply own things for the practical uses they have – their *utility* value. He points out how we also seek to own things for the value they have for us as *symbols* of who we would like others to think we are. Though there might be a certain utility advantage for the Rolls Royce owner in terms of the extra comfort the car affords him or her, at least as important is its value as a *status symbol*. It symbolises or expresses the resources, and, by implication, the importance, of its owner. The same goes for the possession of mink coats, diamonds, enormous houses in particular residential areas, and so forth.

Kula valuables similarly enable Trobrianders and their neighbours to gain prestige. But they do so in a rather different way. In the kula there is no advantage or prestige attached to *keeping* a valuable. You receive the admiration of others for two reasons. First, because *you* were chosen by your partner to be the recipient of the valuable article, rather than any other of his partners. Second, because you can show yourself to be generous by *giving it away* again in turn. As Malinowski (1922) puts it:

> Ownership . . . in [the] kula, is quite a special economic relation. A man who is in the kula never keeps any article for longer than, say, a year or two. Even this exposes him to the reproach of being niggardly . . . on the other hand, each man has an enormous number of articles passing through his hands during his lifetime, of which he enjoys a temporary possession, and which he keeps in trust for a time. The possession hardly ever makes him use the articles, and he remains under the obligation soon again to hand them on to one of his partners. But the temporary ownership allows him to draw a great deal of renown, to exhibit his article, to tell how he obtained it, and to plan to whom he is going to give it.

Here, then, social honour is not attached to the acquisition in order to possess. The purpose of wanting to acquire is not to own, but to give away again. In Malinowski's words: ' . . . a man who owns a thing is naturally expected to share it, to distribute it, to be its trustee and dispenser . . . the main symptom of being powerful is to be wealthy and of wealth is to be generous . . . the more important he is, the more will he desire to shine by his generosity . . .'

It would appear that here we have the answer to the kula. It is a system of 'conspicuous generosity', to parody Veblen. It is a way of allowing people to gain importance and to be seen to be important. Status-seeking is not the prerogative of the materialist West. The Trobrianders wish to be thought of as important and powerful too – they just use different ways to do it. From the point of view of individual Trobrianders this is almost certainly the whole story. For them, the kula is an institution geared to the pursuit of status. But is their story the only one about the kula that needs to be told? After all, they learnt to kula; it existed before they did. Since they did not invent it, can we rely only on their views of what it is about? The functionalist in Malinowski will not allow him to stop here. He also wants to know why the kula is necessary for the Trobriand social system. He wants to know what the kula *does* – what its function is.

The answers that Malinowski and later functionalist analysts of his material give run along these lines: because many kula exchanges take place between partners who live on islands many miles apart, its existence allows economic and political relationships to take place between people who would otherwise never meet. The result is a greater economic and political integration of the whole of Trobriand society, and of different societies with each other, than would otherwise have been possible.

## The economic function of the kula

Though kula partners are not allowed to engage in ordinary trading with one another, non-partners are. Thus an expedition of a large number of members from one island to another will not simply result in kula exchanges. Between men who are not kula partners, bartering for non-kula goods is quite normal. According to Malinowski (1922), this is an important *latent* function of the kula. It makes trading relations possible between people who would otherwise never come into contact with one another, for their mutual economic benefit. 'Side by side with the ritual exchange of arm-shells and necklaces, the natives carry on ordinary trade, bartering from one island to another a great number of utilities, often improcurable in the district to which they are imported and indispensable there.'

Here, then, is an economic function of the kula of which members would either be unaware, or certainly consider of secondary importance to the kula exchanges. In contrast, for functionalists it is such *unintended* consequences of people's activities which are usually of the greatest importance to identify.

## The political function of the kula

It is the fact that the kula makes possible such long-distance social interaction, embracing the whole of Trobriand society and linking the Trobrianders with more distant tribal societies, that functionalists have usually pounced on as its key. Two excerpts from *Argonauts of the Western Pacific* give a flavour of the kula's political function which is identified by Malinowski (1922) himself:

> An average man has a few partners near by . . . and with these partners he is generally on very friendly terms . . . the overseas partner is, on the other hand, a host, patron and ally in a land of danger and insecurity.
>
> The kula is thus an extremely big and complex institution . . . It welds together a considerable number of tribes, and it embraces a vast complex of activities, inter-connected and playing into one another, so as to form one organic whole.

Malinowski's functionalism and the integrative consequences of the kula (which he sees as so central to its significance) are clearly apparent here. In a later study of Malinowski's data, J. Singh Uberoi (1962) argued that the integrative function of the kula is even more fundamental than Malinowski himself acknowledged. His thesis is this. Only kula objects among valuable things are owned by individuals, rather than by groups of kin. Only in the kula do people enter into relations as individuals rather than as representatives of their kin groups. Only in the kula is self-interest, rather than group-interest, the motivating force.

How does this reduction in the importance of kinship relations in the kula allow it to enable a great political *integration* of the whole community? Uberoi argues that because the kula enables people to be released from obligations to their kin groups, they are better able to perceive Trobriand society as a wider whole. Rather in the way that the totem tells the Arunta about the wider society on which they ultimately depend, the kula encourages the Trobrianders to think of their society as a whole, rather than as a collection of competing kin groups. This is how Uberoi (1962) puts it:

> The kula extends the political society beyond the district by periodically depreciating the ties which bind an individual to the other members of his own local lineage or district, and re-emphasising his obligations towards his kula partner, who belongs to an otherwise opposed district . . . on a kula expedition . . . each individual . . . stands by and for himself, released from the normal restraints of group solidarity; but because he pursues his individual

self-interest through wooing his kula partner, he stands not only for himself, but also for the whole chain of partners which goes to make up the kula ring . . . [the kula valuables symbolise to] the normally kin-bound individuals . . . the highest point of their individual self-interest [and also] the interest of the widest political association of which they all partake [the kula].

This is a typical functionalist analysis. The accounts of activities by the people involved in them are forgotten. The interest is in what *good* an institutionalised activity does, or has done, for the society as a whole. The assumption is that an institution would not exist unless it was necessary. The observer's job is to see *why* it is necessary, what *function* it is performing. The Trobriander sails to distant islands to pursue his self-interest and to maximise his prestige. Unknown to him, but perfectly apparent to the perceptive functionalist, is the fact that he is *really* integrating his society, both economically and politically.

## SOCIAL CHANGE

So far, so good. Here we have an explanation of the source of individual happiness and societal health. However, the problem of social change has to be addressed:
(a) not only do functionalists have to take account of the fact that change *does* occur in societies, but also;
(b) the idea of modernity – the modern ideal – is that knowledge is supposed to provide humans with the chance to create a *good* society and that change can represent progress, a good thing.

The functionalist is faced with a problem here, though. The functionalist model of the individual is the structural-consensus one of a determined, constrained, regulated social actor, whose choices are created for him or her by socialisation. To be modernist, and allow that social change and social reconstruction can be actively promoted, and achieved, by social actors – that people can create society – turns the relationship between the individual and society on its head. The functionalist way around this is to use the organismic analogy again, and to say that social progress occurs as it does with organisms – as *evolutionary* change.

Change takes the form of *structural differentiation*. As Bilton *et al.* (1987) say:

Just as the evolution of animals produces more sophisticated specialised organs to perform particular functions for the whole creature [so differentiation means] society comes to develop a range of distinct institutions which deal more adequately with particular needs of the social whole.

. . . differentiation is a type of splitting or separation of a previously undivided unit. The new units created by this process differ from the earlier unit by being more specialised in the functions they perform. The two new units differ from each other since they are structured in such a way that each of them can perform unique functions that the other unit cannot. . . .

This emphasis on differentiation is apparent in Talcott Parsons' twentieth-century approach to social change. Institutions change, says Parsons, if the needs of the system change. The rise of industrialisation in modern societies has proved the major impetus to family change, for a new industrial economy requires a new form of family to perform new, specialist functions. This need is met by a process of differentiation, thus ensuring evolution and progress. In Parsons' (1966) own words:

The kinship-organised household in predominantly [traditional, non-industrial] society is *both* the unit of residence and the primary unit of agricultural production. In [industrial] societies, however, most productive work is performed in specialised units, such as workshops, factories or offices manned by people who are *also* members of family households. Thus two sets of roles and collectives have become differentiated and their functions separated.

This splitting-off of the nuclear family household from production does not mean the family has *lost* significance however. After all, it is evolution – progress and improvement. The loss of the economic function to specialised workplaces means the new, non-productive household can concentrate on performing non-economic functions better than the dual-purpose, peasant household could. The removal of economic activity from the home means family members can pay more time and attention to each other: thus the emotional quality of the relationship between adult family members is enhanced, and more effort is put into the socialisation of children. The social system benefits: 'these developments enhance the significance of the family as provider of a secure emotional base for its members' participation in society' (Parsons, 1971). At the same time, now that production takes place in locations specifically designed for this alone, the performance of this economic function is also superior. Once again, the social system benefits; through evolution, then, modern societies forge ahead.

So, just as social structures have the character they do – not because of the purposive intentions of individuals, but because of system needs – so social change occurs, not because people want to have it, but because of evolution. The analogy with the organism therefore explains both social structure and social change; functionalism can be a theory extolling the virtues of modernity, while still seeing the individual as a societal creation.

Functionalism has exerted a tremendous influence on sociology. As we noted at the beginning of the chapter, for much of the first half of this century it occupied a largely unchallenged theoretical position in the subject. Through the influence of anthropology in Britain, and of Talcott Parsons and his supporters in America, by the middle of the century sociology came to be more or less synonymous with functionalist sociology. Other theoretical approaches were kept well in the background. The sociological enterprise was seen as principally concerned with a search for the 'real' significance of social institutions – the contribution they make to the maintenance of the social systems in which they are found. Because its influence has substantially waned today, it is easy to be over-critical of the rather narrow vision of functionalism's adherents. Now it seems rather strange that during functionalism's ascendancy, so little attention should have been paid to relations of dominance and subordination, advantage and disadvantage in society. It also seems self-evident that humans must be recognised as more than just 'cultural dopes', obediently learning sets of cultural prescriptions for action so that their social systems can persist. Today it seems clear that sociology must take account of the interpretive abilities of people in order to properly understand their actions.

In our eagerness to demonstrate the errors and partialities in functionalism/structural-consensus theory, we must not forget to acknowledge the contribution this kind of theory has made to sociology. The unintended social consequences of people's beliefs and actions *are* important to recognise. Sociology *does* have an important revelatory task. It *is* necessary sometimes to go beyond people's own explanations for their actions in order to properly understand social behaviour. This is undoubtedly functionalism's contribution. Nevertheless, we would also be quite wrong to deny functionalism's weaknesses. Four main ones are usually identified. It is argued that functionalism:

(a) has an inherent tendency to 'reify' society;

(b) is not able to explain social change adequately;

39

(c)  is based upon an oversocialised view of human beings;
(d)  does not take enough account of power and conflict in society.

FUNCTIONALISM AND THE 'REIFICATION' OF SOCIETY

Functionalists explain the existence of institutionalised patterns of behaviour and belief in terms of the good effects these have for the social system in which they are found. Institutions are not the product of decisions made by individuals, since they exist prior to these individuals. The problem of social order is not how human beings can create an ordered society. It is how social systems can create social beings, socialised into conforming to institutionalised rules of behaviour necessary for their existance. The insistence that societies acquire their functioning characteristics prior to the existence of their members leaves a rather awkward question, however. If *people* do not decide what is functional for their society, then who *does* decide? The functionalist seems to be left with the proposition that the social system itself decides what is good for it. Yet this is clearly absurd. Societies cannot think; only people can. This is known as the problem of *'reification'*. Functionalists seem to 'reify' society – to treat it as a thing – by endowing it with the ability to think and act intentionally that only humans have.

FUNCTIONALISM AND SOCIAL CHANGE

Functionalism seems to promote a static and conservative picture of society. The functionalist position is that institutions continue to exist because they are functional – they are satisfying a need of the social system. The job of the sociologist is to reveal what the good effects of particular institutions are. This seems to come remarkably close to *automatically* justifying what the status quo in a particular society happens to be; it seems to imply that all persisting social arrangements in a society *must* be beneficial, otherwise they would not remain in existence. When the problem of social change *is* addressed, it is seen as evolutionary, benign and adaptive; a slow process, whereby the social system accommodates new circumstances. This leaves the theory unable to explain rapid, disruptive change – politically inspired innovation dramatically overturning existing structures. The events in Eastern Europe in 1989, 1990 and 1991 could hardly be addressed by using the functionalist notion of change as organic adaptation.

FUNCTIONALISM AND SOCIALISATION

As we said in Chapter 1, *action* theories have crucial objections to the functionalist/structural-consensus model. For them, the real criticism of functionalism is that it over-emphasises socialisation as an explanation of social behaviour. The interpretive emphasis of action theory is that people are not passive recipients of cultural recipes for social action. Among living things, humans alone are able to *choose* how to act. Far from being a simple reflection of cultural prescription, such choices are made in the light of how people see the world – particularly how they interpret the actions of others. Social action is thus *voluntary* action. It is action chosen in the light of the actor's interpretation of reality.

FUNCTIONALISM, POWER AND CONFLICT

As we also saw in Chapter 1, the criticism *structural-conflict* theory makes of the functionalist/consensus approach to social life has two elements. First, according to conflict theory, functionalism fails to take account of the influence on behaviour of society's structures of inequality. The argument here is that people are not only influenced by the norms and values of the culture into which they are socialised. Their social lives are also crucially influenced by the advantages they possess; there are practical, as well as normative, constraints on behaviour which bring the advantaged and the disadvantaged into conflict. Second, for conflict theorists, functionalism is based on a fundamentally flawed conception of the role of socialisation into cultural rules. In any conflict theory, norms and values only have the character they do because their role is to obscure, as well as to legitimate, the facts of inequality in society. Far from socialisation being the instrument of social order and cohesion, it is a mechanism of power and control.

# CONCLUSION

It was not until the 1960s that these sorts of criticisms caused functionalism to lose its influence. Alternative theoretical approaches came to be considered attractive and, indeed, superior. It was at this time that changes in their experiences altered people's perceptions of modern society, and sociologists were no exception. This was the decade of social reappraisal. The smug complacency encouraged by the economic prosperity of the 1950s, when Prime Minister Harold Macmillan confidently proclaimed that his British constituents had 'never had it so good,' was replaced in the 1960's by a genuine concern for social justice and a real awareness of inequality and deprivation. Poverty had been 'rediscovered', both in Britain and the USA.

The Civil Rights movement in America began to demand equality for Blacks. The feminist movement began to demand equality for women. US imperialism – most notoriously in Vietnam – was denounced by many in the Western world. In such a context, where social change was being demanded and conflict between different groups in society was clearly apparent, functionalism began to be seen more and more as remote from the real world. As a theory which sets out to explain the benefits of social institutions, to reveal the mechanisms by which social systems achieve cohesion and integration, and to show how they persist, it seemed hardly relevant or adequate in a world where many had begun to see *disadvantage* and *inequality*, where conflict and a lack of social cohesion were clearly apparent, and where social change seemed necessary. In such circumstances it is not surprising that alongside the emergence of interpretive alternatives to functionalism, another kind of alternative theory, which *does* explain conflict, confront change, and attempt to predict the future, should have proved intellectually appealing to many. We will look at this theory in the next chapter.

# CHAPTER THREE

# *Marx and Marxism*

Like functionalism, Marxism is a theory designed to promote the good society. Like functionalism, it is a *response* to modernity, and, like functionalism, it is a *part* of modernity – it is part of the modern belief that societies can be transformed for the better, that progress can be achieved in social organisation through the application of human knowledge. Like functionalism, Marxism rests upon the belief that the potential for individual fulfilment and freedom is linked inextricably to the potential for progress in social organisation – to the structure of society. There the similarity ends.

According to Marx, the potential for individual fulfilment is linked to the economic or productive activity of a society; in particular, the opportunity to be free in modern society is only possible when the class-based productive system characteristic of capitalism is abolished.

Can this progress be achieved? The need is for people to come to realise the truth of Marxist theory – to realise that liberation depends upon the destruction of capitalism. Once they know that the key to freedom lies here, they will use it to unlock the door – they will take political action to abolish classes.

How can they be made to see the truth and take action? This is the key problem, for what they think is the truth about the world is manipulated. In capitalism, as in all class societies, prevailing beliefs will deny the truth that class-based production prevents freedom by:
(a) legitimising such systems of production and their consequences;
(b) preventing people from recognising evidence of lack of freedom.

However, according to Marx, capitalism has within it the seeds of its own destruction. The activity of producing goods in this system will, over time, inevitably produce consequences which will cause so much misery that false beliefs will be discarded and people will come to realise the truth of Marxist theory and the real facts of their social circumstances. Then, armed with the truth, they will act, change society and become free.

## MARX AND HISTORICAL MATERIALISM

In Marxist theory the most important human activity is *economic activity* – the production of material goods. In a speech at Marx's graveside, Engels said that 'Mankind must first of all eat, drink, have shelter and clothing, before it can pursue politics, science, art, religion, etc.' (1976).

According to Marx (1976), understanding the way a society organises its production is the key to understanding the whole of its social structure. The Marxist view is that 'the production of the means of subsistence . . . forms the foundation upon which the state institutions, the legal conceptions, art and even the ideas on religion, of the people concerned have been evolved.'

For Marx, social structures are not randomly created. He argues that there is a quite definite pattern to the way societies in different parts of the world, and at different times in history, have organised the production of material goods. This theory of history and society is called *historical materialism*. For our purposes we can identify its following elements.

First, all societies that have existed or do exist today exhibit one of five different ways of organising production. These different ways of producing goods Marx called *modes of production*. The five are (in chronological order) the *primitive communist, ancient, feudal, capitalist* and *communist* modes.

Second, apart from the first and last modes of production – the primitive communist and communist modes – each mode has one crucial characteristic in common. Each is a way of producing goods based on *classes*. Though the term 'class' has different uses elsewhere in sociology (and all sorts of uses in speech) the Marxist usage is a quite specific one. According to Marx, in all non-communist societies – in the ancient, feudal and capitalist modes – there are just two classes that matter. There is the class that *owns* the means of production – it is their property – and there is the class that does not own it.

In systems of production based on classes, goods are produced in a quite definite way. The majority of people, who do not own the means of production, do the productive work for the benefit of those – the minority – who do own it. In Marxist theory, this is the key feature of non-communist societies at any time in history. The production of material goods (the most important activity of humans, remember), *always* takes place by means of the *exploitation* of the labour of the majority, non-property-owning class by the minority class, which owns the means of production and does not work. That is, the relationship between classes is a *conflict* relationship.

44

There are no classes in either of the communist modes. In primitive communist societies people cannot produce a surplus. This is usually because of an inhospitable environment, or a lack of technological know-how, or a combination of the two. Because such peoples only produce enough to allow them to exist at subsistence level, everyone has to work. There is no surplus property, and there is therefore no possibility for classes to emerge to exploit it. In the communist mode there are no classes because private property has been abolished – people are not able to own the means of production.

Because in any class-based mode of production goods are produced in this exploitative way, in Marxist writing the owners of the means of production are usually called the *dominant* class, while the non-owning, exploited class which performs the productive work is called the *subordinate* class.

According to Marx, the history of human society is the history of different kinds of productive systems based on class exploitation. He says we can divide up the history of any society into different *epochs* or ages, each of which is dominated by one particular mode of production, with its own characteristic class relationships. All societies will eventually pass through all these stages in history and all will eventually become communist. However, not all societies evolve at the same rate. This is why at any particular time in history different societies exhibit different modes of production – they are at different stages of historical development.

What distinguishes different modes of production from one another? All non-communist modes have in common the production of goods by means of the domination and exploitation of one class by another. What is different in each case is who the classes are. Each non-communist mode of production has a different, dominant, property-owning class and a different subordinate, exploited, non-property-owning class. Furthermore, each mode grows out of the death of the previous one.

THE ANCIENT MODE OF PRODUCTION

The oldest form of class production – hence its name – is the ancient mode of production. This mode grew out of the subsistence primitive communist mode primarily because of technological improvements. For example, in the Iron Age humans developed productive techniques which allowed specialist animal farming and settled agricultural production. This in turn enabled the production of a surplus, and allowed a more complex division of labour than was possible in a purely subsistence economy. In effect, a dominant class of *non-producers* could emerge.

The distinguishing feature of this mode of production is that people are owned as productive property by other, more powerful people. That is, it is production based on *slavery*. Here then, there is a dominant class of *masters* and a subordinate class of *slaves*. Production takes place by means of the involuntary labour of people who are owned as property by others.

Ancient Greece and Rome provide the classic examples of slavery as a mode of production. In the Greek and Roman empires about a third of the population was enslaved. Most had entered into slavery as prisoners-of-war, following battles undertaken as part of the imperialist (empire-building) policies of the Greek and Roman states.

One of the main reasons why the ancient mode of production disintegrated was that the state power upon which it depended became eroded. As it became more and more difficult for the ancient states to control and coerce people living in distant parts of their empires, so did the possibility of sustaining slavery as a mode of production.

THE FEUDAL MODE OF PRODUCTION

In place of the ancient mode of production emerged a new mode of a much more local character, called feudalism. Feudal production was based upon the ability of warriors or nobles controlling small local territories by force of arms to coerce and exploit an agricultural labour force. In feudalism the dominant class controls the land, and comprises the *lords*. The subordinate class is made up of *serfs*. Production takes place by means of the labour of those who *have* to work the land in order to survive. Since these labourers do not own the land, but are merely tenants on it, they are obliged to give up much of the product of their labour as rent (in the form of a 'fee' called a *tithe*) to the landlords.

Feudalism dominated Europe from the Dark Ages until early modern times. Two factors in particular heralded its death and helped to usher in a new mode of production, based on a new form of class exploitation. First, strongly centralised political power was re-established in Europe not in the form of large, unwieldy empires, but in the form of absolutist monarchies. This allowed sufficient state control to be exercised within national territories in European countries for proper legal systems to be devised and enforced. This, in turn, provided an opportunity for economic activity to extend beyond local feudal boundaries, and for widespread trade to become possible, for example through the gradual unification of tax and currency systems within major trading areas, and along major trading routes such as the Rhine.

Second, as a result of the changes brought about by the agricultural revolution, agricultural production became rationalised and more efficient. One of the most significant consequences of this was the *Enclosures Acts*. These Acts denied the bulk of the agricultural labour force the subsistence rights over the strips of land they had been entitled to under feudalism. Replaced by sheep, and by non-labour-intensive farming using machines, these labourers were made landless. Marx (1976) described it in *Capital*, 'Sheep ate men'. Thrown off the land, and with no other means of subsistence than their *labour power*, workers were forced to sell their labour to employers for a wage. A *labour market* thus emerged for the first time.

## THE CAPITALIST MODE OF PRODUCTION

Production now took on a new class character. The labour power of a class of landless labourers – a *proletariat*, as Marxists call them – could now be purchased for a wage by a class of property-owning employers – for whom the Marxist term is the *bourgeoisie*.

So capitalism developed in Britain before industrialisation; *agricultural* goods were produced first of all in a capitalistic way. It was only later, when factories were built and industrial machines were developed, that *industrial* capitalism became established and an *urban* proletariat emerged.

In capitalist society, the bourgeoisie are the dominant class because, like the masters in slave societies and the lords in feudal societies, they own the productive wealth – the means of production.

During the development of capitalism, the character of property in which capitalists have invested their wealth has, of course, altered. In the early stages of capitalism, as we have just noted, productive property primarily took the form of *land*, with the proletariat earning wages as agricultural labourers on it. Later, *industrial* production gave rise to capitalist investment in *factories* and *machines*, with the proletariat earning wages as industrial manual labourers. Still later, capitalism took on the form typical of contemporary industrial capitalism. Today, instead of actually owning and controlling industrial production themselves, the ownership of productive property usually takes the form of *capital investment in stocks and shares*. (Of course, capitalist land-owners, and owners and controllers of their own enterprises – especially the smaller ones – still exist in plenty today.)

Despite these alterations to the nature of productive property in capitalist society, for Marxists the character of class relations between owners of property and non-owners of property is essentially the same as in earlier, class-based modes of production. Though the bourgeoisie do not make goods themselves, they nevertheless own the means of production. For this reason, they will always profit from the difference between the cost to them of the labour of the proletariat, and the value of the goods produced by the proletariat's labour power. The important fact is that workers will *always* be paid less than the value of the goods they produce. If this did not happen, the system could not work; without profit, reinvestment of this surplus into the productive power of capitalism would not take place, and enterprises would wither and die in the face of competition. This *surplus value* costs the capitalist nothing, and is a tangible symbol of the exploitation of wage-earners' labour power by employers. Though not as obvious as the exaction of tithes by feudal lords, or the ownership of people by slave-owners, the relationship between the capitalist and the wage-earner is of exactly the same kind. In Marx's (1976) words, 'The history of all hitherto existing society is the history of class struggle.'

## THE ROLE OF THE SUPERSTRUCTURE

So far, our account of Marxist theory has concentrated on production – on economic relationships. What about the rest of social life? The defining characteristic of Marxist sociology is the view that economic activity is the architect which designs the character of other aspects of life.

In order to convey this, Marx calls the way a society organises production its *base,* or *infrastructure*; economic activity, that is, is the basis of all else in that society. The rest of its social organisation – its non-economic activities and its ideas, beliefs and philosophies – he calls its *superstructure.* The use of these terms is important. It stresses the way in which a society's superstructure is created by its base; one set of activities is built upon the other.

### INSTITUTIONS

First, at the level of social structure, non-economic institutions in any epoch are always organised in such a way as to benefit the mode of production. The task of the sociologist is to analyse this, as in the following accounts of the family and of education in capitalist society (Bilton *et al.* 1987):

*The Family*

Most Marxist analyses draw attention to the ways in which families tend to encourage and reproduce hierarchical inegalitarian relationships, and to act as a safety-valve, dampening down discontent so that it is robbed of revolutionary content. In providing a place where children can be conceived, born and reared in relative safety, the family is providing tomorrow's labour force. At the same time, by offering a centre for relaxation, recreation, refreshment and rest, the family helps to ensure that members of today's labour force are returned to work each day with their capacity to work renewed and strengthened. This is what is meant when it is said that the family reproduces labour power on a generational as well as a daily basis.

## Education

Bowles and Gintis argue that schooling operates within the 'long shadow of work': that is, the education system reflects the organisation of production in capitalist society. For example, the fragmentation of most work processes is mirrored in the breaking up of the curriculum into tiny 'packages' of knowledge, each subject divorced from all others; lack of control over work processes is reflected in the powerlessness of pupils with regard to what they will learn in school or how they will learn it; and the necessity of working for pay when jobs seem pointless and unfulfilling in themselves is paralled by the emphasis in schools on learning in order to gain good grades, rather than learning for its own sake. Therefore, Bowles and Gintis claim there is a *correspondence* between the nature of work in capitalist societies, and the nature of schooling.

This interest in analysing the ways in which the character of non-economic institutions benefits the system of production has a close parallel with functionalism. As with functionalism, the analysis of an institution takes the form of identifying its positive role in the system; the above accounts of the benefits for capitalism of family life and schooling could quite legitimately be said to be the identification of the 'function' that the institutions perform in meeting the needs of capitalism. Though both are 'systemic' theories, the crucial difference concerns the way they characterise the system, and whose needs are being met by it.

IDEOLOGIES

At the level of ideas, the relationship between the base and the superstructure is apparent in the way the prevailing beliefs in any epoch also support the organisation of production. This is especially important in societies where the activity of producing goods involves the exploitation of the bulk of the population, rendering them grossly unequal and disadvantaged. While the compliance of the subordinate class in this arrangement *can* be secured by physical force, in the Marxist view the most effective way they can be persuaded to acquiesce in their own subordination is via what they think – their *ideas* and *beliefs*. What is distinctive about a Marxist approach to the world of ideas in a class society is its interest in the *ideological* nature of beliefs. As we said earlier, for Marxists, ideologies are systems of belief which:

(a) legitimate the class-based system of production by making it appear right and just, and/or

(b) obscure the reality of its consequences from the gaze of the people.

Here again there are parallels with functionalism. Just as conformity to shared ideas is the fundamental functionalist source of cohesion and order, so Marxists conceive of class societies persisting due to the commitment of individuals to the same ideological beliefs; here however, socialisation determines what people think for the benefit of the property-owning class, and the maintenance of the system.

According to Marxists, the *dominant* ideas, beliefs and values in a class society (which are ideas about which there is most agreement), are not there by chance. They act as ideologies, propping up a structure which, without such ideological support, would collapse. Marxists argue that although from time to time dominant classes *do* have to resort to naked force to maintain their power and supremacy, the absence of such obvious coercion should not be taken to signify an absence of exploitation. On the contrary, they suggest, all a lack of naked oppression can ever indicate is a lack of opposition, and the lack of any need to use force. It does not mean that domination is not taking place. It is only that the dominated are unaware of their condition, because of the effectiveness of the ideologies into which they have been socialised.

How do such dominant ideas gain general acceptance? Like functionalists, Marxists argue that particular ideas prevail through various key agencies of socialisation. In contemporary society, for example, both Marxists and functionalists would point to the important role played by institutions like the family, the education system and the mass media in promoting generally held beliefs and values. The essential difference between functionalists and Marxists concerns their interpretations of the role of the socialisation process that such institutions ensure. For functionalists, it is the way we learn ideas that we need to know in order to think and behave in the ways required of us by the social system. For Marxists, it is the way we learn those ideas which serves to hide from our eyes, or justify, the real character of a class society.

For both theories there *is* a prevailing culture which people learn through socialisation. The difference between them concerns the job this culture does. For functionalists, it ensures social integration. For Marxists, it ensures social inequality and domination.

We can look at some prevailing ideas in contemporary capitalist Britain to see how a Marxist would explain their superstructural significance. From the Marxist viewpoint, any ideas in Britain which, for example:

(a) divert people's attention away from the reality of class inequality;
(b) reproduce demand for goods by encouraging consumerism;
(c) encourage the wage-earning class to accept their subordinate role;
(d) justify the inequality between the classes

all help to perpetuate capitalism in this society. How is this done? How do such ideas come to prevail? A Marxist approach to the superstructure of contemporary Britain might be as follows.

### Diversionary institutions

Capitalist production is exploitative, according to Marxists. A major reason for its survival is that institutions exist to divert the attention of the exploited away from the reality of their condition. One important vehicle for doing this is the *entertainment industry*. For example, much *popular music*, with its characteristic emphasis on the attractions of romantic love and/or sexual satisfaction as the pinnacle of human fulfilment hardly aims to shed light on the reality of class exploitation! Nor does much *popular literature*, not only by its emphasis on sex/love. Escapism of other kinds abounds: the never-ending production of gangster/detective novels, war novels, science fiction, and so on, bears testimony to this preoccupation. A substantial proportion of *television and radio programmes* has similar consequences. From situation comedies to quiz games, from soap operas to cops and robbers films, such entertainment promotes a trivialisation of reality. Programmes like these create 'pretend' worlds, where the facts of life in a class society are ignored (see pp. 61–2).

The *family* can also perform a similar task. A dominant belief in contemporary society is that individual emotional satisfaction can only be found in marriage and child-rearing. However pleasant or otherwise the successful accomplishment of such goals may be, we must realise that the pursuit of such an achievement renders a desire for fulfilment through other activities, like work, less likely. The result is that exploited, meaningless work is tolerated. Life becomes about the achievement of marital and parental satisfaction, in order to compensate. As a Ford car worker told Huw Beynon (1973) 'I just close my eyes, stick it out, and think of the wife and kids.'

Much of the *news media* perform an important diversionary role in capitalist society too. For example, tabloid newspapers like the *Sun*, the *Star*, the *Daily Mirror*, the *Daily Mail* and the *Daily Express*, traditionally concentrate on the trivial, the sensational and the titillating rather than on a serious reporting of events. This *deliberate* suppression and distortion of reality can only further encourage people living in a capitalist society to divert their gaze away from inequality, deprivation and exploitation. Indeed, since it is only through mass media that we gain most of our information about reality, a failure to provide such information is not only diversionary. It also means we are being provided with a picture of the world that is false.

## Consumerism: the reproduction of demand

Capitalism depends on the reproduction of demand. Any social institution which promotes the purchase of goods perpetuates their production by capitalist means. Clearly, the main way in which we are encouraged to consume is by means of *advertising*. Whether on television and radio, or in the cinema, in newspapers and magazines or on billboards, advertisements glorify the possession of material goods (compare this with the values underpinning the kula) and thereby promote their acquisition.

The family helps reproduce demand too. In Western societies, many people live in nuclear families – the smallest kind of family unit. Each family is economically independent, purchasing its own goods. This ensures that demand is maximised. In larger households, demand for consumer goods would decrease.

## The acquiescence of wage-earners in their subordination

Capitalism depends on the bulk of the population being socialised into accepting a subordinate role. Once again, the family plays an important part. It is in the family that we first learn the meaning of authority and obedience. Learning to submit to the wishes of parents provides just the training necessary to cope with being a wage-earner and under the authority of an employer. *Education* obviously reinforces this training.

*The justification of inequality*

Capitalism depends on its inherent inequalities, if recognised, being accepted as just. It is in the classroom that we first encounter the inevitability of inequality. Here we learn that people do not only possess *different* abilities. They possess *better* or *worse* abilities. 'Clever' children succeed and are rewarded with good grades and exam results. 'Less able' children deserve poorer rewards. What better training for life in a society where different abilities are also judged as superior and inferior, and judged accordingly? Experiences in school can only encourage people to believe that inequality of reward is just. Such beliefs are expressed in such commonly held views as these: 'Of course doctors should be paid more than dustmen. They do a much more important job.' The unequal distribution of rewards among different occupations reflects their importance. Or again 'Anyone could be a dustman. Only able/intelligent/skilled people can become doctors.' Achievement within an unequal world reflects merit.

In a fundamental way, then, education, with its intrinsic emphasis on competition and selection, on success and failure, on merit and de-merit, teaches members of a capitalist society the justice of inequality. In particular, it teaches the 'less able' – the 'failures' – to expect, and accept, low rewards in their lives.

Marxists argue that such an analysis of the relationship between the infrastructure and the superstructure tells us a great deal about *power* in a class society. The dominant class rules, but not by necessarily being the actual office-holders who make decisions. It rules because its interests are considered superior by all those – property-owners and propertyless alike – who have been subject to socialisation into dominant ideas by superstructural agencies. In Marx's (1976) words: 'The ideas of the ruling class are, in every age, the ruling ideas.'

It is for these reasons that the concepts of *false consciousness* and *class consciousness* are of such importance in Marxist theory. Because the subordinate class subscribe to dominant ideologies, which obscure the real nature of class society from its gaze, its picture of the world and its place in it is wrong. Its consciousness of reality is false.

Only when a class-based mode of production falters will members of a subordinate class start to discard their false images of the world, and come to see the reality of their exploited status. Then they come to see themselves as they really are – a class. In Marx's words, they develop *class consciousness*. Their *subjective* view of themselves and their condition comes to match its *objective* reality. It is the emergence of class consciousness in a subordinate class that is the key which unlocks the revolution which overthrows a mode of production and its dominant class. How does this happen? How does false consciousness become class consciousness?

As with the existence of false ideas, true consciousness cannot come into being independently of economic circumstances. According to Marx, the impetus for revolution does not arise randomly, or by chance. Ideas about how a society ought to be restructured can only develop under certain circumstances. In particular, when institutional arrangements (which have come into being to support a particular mode of production) no longer suit productive relationships, because of the alterations these have undergone through time, pressure for change builds up. The exploited class then embark on a political struggle, designed to replace old social arrangements with ones more suited to new economic arrangements.

## SOCIAL CHANGE

### FEUDALISM TO CAPITALISM

In feudal society, the owners of land were the dominant class, owning the dominant means of production. The superstructure supported their dominance, and ideas that reflected their class interests were the ruling ideas. For example, feudal law bound serfs to the land, and political power was in the hands of landlords and nobles. Feudal religion legitimated these arrangements. As one Victorian hymn puts it, three hundred years later:

> The rich man at his castle,
> The poor man at his gate:
> God made them high or lowly,
> And ordered their estate.

For the Marxist, there is nothing surprising in the correspondence between the characteristics of production and the character of prevailing ideas. Clearly, if feudal legal, political or religious ideas had stressed something different, feudal production could not have survived. The correspondence between the material world and the world of ideas continued as economic change took place. As capitalism replaced feudalism, superstructural ideas necessarily changed in consequence, in order to support and justify the *new* economic arrangements, so that *they* could work. According to the Marxist, this is how this happened. As feudalism progressed, technological innovations began to transform the nature of production, from labour-intensive agriculture to mechanised

54

agriculture, and ultimately to industrial production. As these agricultural and industrial revolutions unfolded, so the new capitalist class emerged as the owners of the foundation of the new and growing means of production – capital.

For a time, however, the superstructure lagged behind these changes, its character still reflecting and legitimating the old economic arrangements. For example, though capitalist production required a mobile labour force and land to be freely available for buying and selling, the old legal and political arrangements prevented this.

Eventually, the strain or contradiction between the interests of the new bourgeoisie and the power and practices of the old land-owning class became too great and the landlord class was overthrown. Though this happened quite quickly and violently in other European societies, the change began earlier, and was more gradual, in Britain. By means of various political alterations which took place over a few centuries, the landlord class came to share political power, first with the capitalist land-owners, and then with the new industrialists. Eventually the control of political decision-making passed irrevocably into capitalist hands, though a residue of influence has remained with the landlords up to today.

CAPITALISM TO COMMUNISM

Marx predicted that the same kind of process would be apparent in the revolutionary transformation of the capitalist mode of production into the communist one. Again, the ideas and actions of the people would be the motor of this change. However, these revolutionary ideas could only come about as a result of the emergence of class consciousness. This would only happen as capitalism developed as a mode of production. According to Marx, the evolution of capitalism can only occur by means of the continual exploitation of the working class. That is, though capitalism survives only by exploiting the wage-earning class to a greater and greater extent, an increase in such exploitation will inevitably transform false consciousness into class consciousness. As a result, the steps which are taken to ensure capitalism's 'progress' as a productive system will, at the same time, guarantee the sowing of the seeds of its own destruction. This is how it is supposed to happen.

As we said earlier, capitalism was established *prior* to the development of industry. But it was only with the *Industrial Revolution*, representing progress for capital, that the reality of capitalist society could start to be visible to its members.

Industrial production created large urban settlements of workers, in similar positions for the first time. Living in the same overcrowded conditions of poverty and squalor, and working in the same factory workplaces, the urban proletariat could together begin to recognise their common exploited state. Furthermore, as capitalism develops as a mode of production, exploitation increases. As this happens, class consciousness begins to replace false consciousness.

Capitalist production depends on capital accumulation. Capitalists accumulate capital by increasing the return from the sale of their goods while at the same time lowering the cost of their production. One major way of lowering costs is to cut labour by constantly mechanising – decreasing the labour force. This has two effects. First, smaller capitalists, lacking the capital to invest in new machinery, are unable to compete successfully. They go to the wall, and join the proletariat class. Second, unemployment increases among the proletariat. Since wage-earners are also consumers, an increase in the impoverishment of some of them reduces demand for goods. Faced with this loss in demand capitalists have to cut costs still further in order to retain profit levels and remain solvent. This is done by either decreasing their labour forces still further or by reducing wage levels. This can be done in two ways. Wages can be *actually* reduced. (The 1926 General Strike took place when miners' wages were reduced.) More topically, they can be 'increased' at a slower rate than the rate of inflation. As a result of either of these methods, demand decreases still further and this further affects supply.

As this process continues, the gap in reward between the contracting bourgeoisie and the ever-growing proletariat increases. As the proletariat become increasingly impoverished in this way, the conditions emerge for the development of a fully-fledged class consciousness among them. The proletariat is thus transformed from merely an *objective* class – a class in fact – to being a *subjective* class – a class in their thoughts – as well. It changes from being just a class *in* itself to being a class *for* itself.

When this class consciousness reaches its fullest extent, the proletariat rise up and overthrow capitalism, taking over the means of production and the state apparatus, as the capitalists did before them.

According to Marx, this is the final revolution in a society. Unlike in earlier revolutions, there will be no new exploiting class. Rule by the proletariat means self-government by the workers. Class society is abolished, with all its evils, and a new realm of human freedom begins in communist society.

Here, at last, is an abundant society where all benefit, and all are free to live and work in a flexible, creative way for *themselves*, rather than for others. People come to control their own destiny and 'make their own history'. Equality brings emancipation. According to Marx (1976) it will be 'possible for me to do one thing today and another tomorrow, to hunt in the morning, fish in the afternoon, rear cattle in the evening, criticise after dinner, *just as I have a mind*, without ever becoming hunter, fisherman, shepherd or critic.'

So, only in communist society can human beings fulfil their potential for creativity and goodness. In all other forms of society, the production of material wealth by the dominance of one class over the rest denies this possibility. Despite the ways it is dressed up by those who have power, in the Marxist view all class societies inevitably *alienate* their members, dehumanise them, and deny them the chance of fulfilling their potential. For Marx, a human being is prevented from being truly human in a class society.

## CONTROVERSIES WITHIN MARXISM

The base/superstructure approach to institutions, ideas, beliefs and social change is what makes Marxist sociology distinctive. According to Lee and Newby (1983) 'This base/superstructure distinction lies at the heart of Marx's sociology . . . Marx himself refers to the base/superstructure distinction as the "guiding thread for my studies"'. Marx wanted to show how non-economic life is directly influenced by the activity of production; how only changes in the economic realm can enable people to see the world as it really is; and therefore how social change is ultimately only possible as a consequence of economic developments. Although revolution has to be undertaken by political action, the realisation of its necessity can only come about as a result of the consequences of economic change. Ideas are therefore, in the end, contingent upon economic circumstances; crucially, *changes* in ideas, involving the shift from false consciousness to class consciousness and therefore the desire to change society, can only come about as a result of economic change. As Marx says (1976) 'Men make their own history, but not under circumstances of their own choosing.'

Ever since these ideas appeared they have caused enormous controversy. One of the most common accusations, according to Lee and Newby (1983), has been that Marx's theory is a theory of *economic determinism* – that it argues that 'all social, political and intellectual development is caused by economic changes and even that all human action is economically motivated.'

Since such a claim is patently untrue, twentieth-century Marxists have insisted that reading Marx this way is to 'vulgarise' Marxism (though they admit, as Marx did himself, that some of Marx's nineteenth-century followers *did* commit such an error; referring to such work, Marx complained 'I am not a Marxist'). Marxists say that Marx certainly did not mean that *at any particular time* the whole of social life is economically determined, or that everyone is always guided by economic motives in their actions. According to Lee and Newby (1983), for Marx such 'economic reductionism' was not historical materialism, and 'neither was Marxism a dehumanizing theory which reduced all individuals to economic automata and denied them any free will.'

Unfortunately, while Marxists agree about what Marx did *not* mean, they do not agree about what he *did* mean. Debates about the *real* meaning of the base/superstructure relationship have dominated twentieth-century Marxist sociology. The problem is that to de-emphasise the economic as the determining influence on ideas is to water down what is distinctively Marxist about Marxism. On the other hand, to assert the economic as the driving influence over the rest of social life certainly makes you distinctively Marxist, but lays you open to charges of economic determinism.

The importance of the debate for Marxists cannot be over-emphasised. This is a modern theory *par excellence*: a set of prescriptions for political action. Here is the blueprint for the creation of the good society; here is the vehicle for human emancipation via societal progress. For the Marxist, the point is not just to *understand* the world, but to *change* it. So it is not just a matter of getting the theory right to *explain* capitalism; the theory *has* to be right, because it is a weapon of political transformation – the purpose of the theory is to *destroy* capitalism.

With this in mind, the fervour and intensity of the debate among twentieth-century Marxists is easily understood. For if Marxism is right, then surely it could be expected that at least some twentieth-century capitalist societies would succumb to the forces of progress specified by the theory? In effect, Marx is saying: 'don't worry, this evil society will ultimately destroy itself. Be patient; perhaps slowly, but nonetheless inexorably, economic developments *will*, in the end, bring the proletariat to realise the truth. Eventually, they *will* act.'

But what is the evidence? As Lee and Newby (1983) put it, modern Marxism has had to come to terms with the occurrence of a non-event:

> In *no* advanced capitalist society has a successful proletarian revolution taken place . . . moreover . . . the most advanced capitalist nation in the world, the United States, appears ostensibly to be almost a living testament to the falsity of some of Marx's predictions. Not only have the majority of American workers persistently increased their standard of living, there is no significant attachment to socialism

among American workers and certainly no widespread revolutionary movement aimed at overthrowing capitalism. In Europe during the 1930s, furthermore, many of the conditions which Marx's writings would lead one to believe would prompt the growth of working class consciousness were present – the widespread immiseration and unemployment of workers in the midst of a severe economic crisis in advanced capitalist societies. The outcome, however, was not the growth of revolutionary socialism within the working class but, equally often, the growth of Fascism . . . the proletariat has persistently failed to act in the ways which Marx both predicted and desired.

Living through such a consolidation of capitalism and confronted by a working class profoundly disinclined to emancipate itself cannot have been easy for twentieth-century Marxists. It is not therefore surprising that the efforts of most of them have been dedicated to making sense of such disillusioning and dispiriting evidence and to modernise Marxism – to try and breathe new political life into the theory.

Two main schools of Marxism emerged:

(a) *humanist Marxism*, whose leading figures were the Italian Antonio Gramsci (1891–1937), and the German members of the Frankfurt school, based in the Frankfurt Institute for Social Research (founded in 1928), whose work is otherwise known as *critical theory*;

(b) *structuralist Marxism*, associated primarily with Frenchman Louis Althusser (1918–1990).

## HUMANIST MARXISM

Humanist Marxists shift the emphasis to the superstructure. For them, twentieth-century political events demonstrate that the ideological locks on the minds of the working class are so secure that the traditional Marxist method of waiting for economic crises to prise them open and precipitate class consciousness and political action should be rethought. The argument is that changes in the base by themselves are insufficient to promote changes in ideas, since under capitalism peoples' minds are too securely held in the distorting grip of ideologies. Theoretically, this means allocating greater importance to the role of the superstructure in explaining the survival of capitalism; politically, it means actively promoting the correct ideas – Marxist theory – to combat ideological indoctrination. However, the Frankfurt school and Gramsci differed over the chances of such superstructural change being effected. Whereas

Gramsci was optimistic, the critical theorists ultimately lost all faith in the revolutionary potential of the working class.


## GRAMSCI


Gramsci is famous for his notion of *hegemony*. He uses this concept to summarise the all-consuming way in which ideologies work to distort a person's view of the world. More than merely referring to the dominance of certain ideas from which capitalism benefits, hegemony conveys the inability of believers even to acknowledge that their beliefs are, in principle, capable of being different, so natural do they take them to be. Describing beliefs as hegemonic, therefore, means indicating that those who subscribe to them take them so much for granted that it requires deliberate and sustained effort to point out their existence, let alone change believers' minds.

Because of this theoretical view of the nature of belief under capitalism, Gramsci was led to insist on the political importance of directly challenging the hegemony of ruling ideas. Gramsci argued that of course Marx was right to say that social change depends on the proletariat seeing the world as it really is. However, he was wrong to assume that this would happen without deliberate action on behalf of the truth. Thus, custodians of the truth (Marxists, with their knowledge of the truth about capitalism) have to become persuaders, preachers and teachers. Before political action can be undertaken to overturn the system, the battle for the *minds* of the soldiers has to be won – bourgeois hegemony has to be deliberately taken on and defeated.

The idea that ideologies have to be exposed, that false consciousness has to be replaced by class consciousness before political action will be taken, is essential to Marxism. What is different with Gramsci is the account of how this will happen. He says it will not happen automatically through economic developments because of the strength of hegemonic beliefs; it has to be deliberately secured through education – by means of counter-socialisation.


## CRITICAL THEORY: THE FRANKFURT SCHOOL

The three main Frankfurt school thinkers were Herbert Marcuse (1898–1979), Theodor Adorno (1903–1969), and Max Horkheimer (1895–1973). Forced to flee Hitler's Germany (in 1933, to the USA) they watched the rise and fall of the Nazi state and then the post-war entrenchment of the capitalist way of life with increasing disillusion. They eventually came to view the emancipation of the working class as a hopeless prospect, principally because of their belief in the immutability of certain superstructural forces which they saw as inexorably suffusing, and dominating, modern life under capitalism. For many thinkers today, the conceptual tools which they used to explain the triumph of capitalism by means of these forces remain highly relevant for an understanding of contemporary life.

Just as Gramsci was concerned to emphasise the control of ideas as the principal source of the power of capital, so critical theory also focuses on instruments of mental domination as the key to capitalism's success. For critical theory, three features of the culture of capitalism in particular function as these instruments:

(1) the way of thinking called 'instrumental reason' – described by Craib (1984) as 'the way of looking at the world which justifies the domination of people over each other and the system over the people';

(2) the role of mass, or popular, culture in stupefying the thought-processes of people, and rendering them incapable of being critical of their world;

(3) the prevalence of a type of personality that not only accepts domination, but actively desires it.

*Instrumental reason* echoes Weber's focus on rationalisation as the key feature of modern life (see Chapter 4). It is intended to convey the predominance of seeing things as instruments – as means to ends – rather than as having value in themselves. It is a focus on *how* things can achieve goals, rather than on whether the goals are worthwhile, or whether the instruments should be used for particular purposes. As Craib (1984) puts it: 'Instrumental reason separates fact and value. It is concerned with how to do things not what should be done.'

The centrality of such reasoning in modern society is in many ways a consequence of capitalist activity, where a preoccupation with new and ever more efficient means of achieving productive ends becomes the be-all and end-all. In this, too, the key role of positivist science in modern life – characterised by a never-ending search for the causes of effects, for technical knowledge of how things produce other things – is crucial; indeed, Marx's own dedication to science as the route to worthwhile knowledge itself eventually came under criticism from the Frankfurt theorists. In summary, for critical theorists, the essence of being human lies in the ability to reason about meaning and value and ultimate good; subverting such potential by encouraging a preoccupation with instrumental reason is thus a crucial means whereby criticism of goals and values embodied in the existing order is likely to be prevented.

The rise of *mass culture* is another major instrument of mental domination identified by the Frankfurt writers. Insisting that an examination of the role of cultural agencies such as popular music, the cinema and radio (writing today they would obviously have included television and videos) is essential for understanding the disinclination of modern humans to do anything but passively acquiesce in their subordination, critical theorists are famous for their contemptuous dismissal of popular entertainment as dehumanising, debasing and worthless. It has led to charges of intellectual snobbery and cultural élitism, but the Frankfurt writers were convinced that the superficiality of low-brow art, and its apparent mission to trivialise reality, is a root cause of the accommodation of the evils of modern society on the part of its members. Indeed, the term critical theory to describe their ideas stems from this view; only intellectuals or artists concerned about, and familiar with, serious and worthy cultural products can escape the shackles and impoverishment of mass entertainment, and be capable of offering a critique of the modern world – to show how a substantially better world *could* be created. This position has also led to criticism of Frankfurt school thinking, since its implications seem to be not only that there are correct values, but that the ability to identify these – to know good and bad when they see it – is a virtue monopolised by the theorists themselves and their followers. Not only do they seem to be claiming that they alone are able to know what is good, but they also seem to be claiming that they alone know what is good for the rest of us – whatever we may think.

The final element in critical theory is an interest in the sort of *personality* characteristics created by the modern world. Marcuse in particular developed this theme, using Freud's ideas to argue that since all societies need to promote the repression, or sublimation, of the desires of their members in order to prevent the collapse of social order in an orgy of individual self-gratification, any proper analysis of modern society must include an examination of how such repression is achieved in *our* sort of world. According to Marcuse, in the early stages of capitalism a high degree of repression is necessary to ensure that people concentrate on work and production. In later, mature, capitalism, however, there is less need for such an exclusive focus, so that the retention of such repression is surplus to the system's requirements. In such circumstances, continuing to insist on such surplus repression from people might well lead to discontent, so psychological pressure is exerted – via what Marcuse calls repressive de-sublimation – to allow us to realise and pursue our desires, but in ways that are useful to the system. Thus, the routine use of sexual images to sell commodities in capitalist societies – cars, cigarettes, alcohol, coffee, clothes, or whatever – is not only sales technique (associating the commodity with an enviable sexual state, or circumstance) but also a way of satisfying desires whose *dis*-satisfaction would be potentially dangerous. As with other forms of human potential, then, for Marcuse, the use of sex in this way takes an integral and profoundly fulfilling part of human existence, and turns it into an instrument of domination or manipulation.

Today, the heir to critical theory analysis is Jürgen Habermas. Though he is generally recognised as one of the major influences on contemporary sociological theorising, to do justice to his ideas here would require a level of exposition incompatible with the introductory aims of this text.

## ALTHUSSER AND STRUCTURALIST MARXISM

For structuralist Marxists like Althusser, humanist Marxism is wrong theory and therefore wrong practice. For Gramsci, human beings are potentially capable of seeing who they have been forced to be by ideologies, and may choose to rid themselves of these hegemonic chains and become who they really are. Like the supporters of other forms of structuralism (see Chapter 7) Althusser rejects completely the idea that humans can be 'subjects' – creative agents – in this way, in charge of their lives and worlds. For him, human life is always entirely structured, and change can only ever come about at the level of a structure whose workings have nothing to do with human cognition, choice and purpose. Althusserian Marxism thus sees itself as the heir to the 'late' Marx – to writings produced towards the end of Marx's life, when he tried to build a scientific analysis of the structure of capitalism – as opposed to the work of the 'young' or 'early' Marx, whose heirs are humanist Marxists like Gramsci, and for whom the way we live is the product of the way we think. Whereas for humanist Marxists social change in capitalist society can only come about through alterations in human purpose and motivation, for Althusser it can only ever happen by change in the structural relations of capitalism.

Theoretically, Althusser is equally opposed to both crude, economistic Marxism and humanist Marxism. Concentrating on the base, on economic organisation to the exclusion of the other structural features of the superstructure, is for him as faulty as concentrating on the *ideas* believed by the working class. Althusser insists it is only scientific Marxism, resting on a proper understanding of the complexity of the structure of capitalism, which can lead to the destruction of such societies.

According to Althusser there are three levels in the stucture of a class society – economic, political and ideological. He defines them broadly, so that they embrace most aspects of human life. The 'economic' concerns all aspects of material production, the 'political' all forms of organisation, and the 'ideological' all kinds of ideas and beliefs. The political level and the ideological level are not the simple creation of the economic. Although the economic level is ultimately the determining level – 'determinant in the last instance' – Althusser defines the political and ideological levels as having 'relative autonomy'. They are thus independent and important in their own right and the interplay between the three levels is complex and varied. Ian Craib (1984) uses a nice architectural analogy to explain this:

We can look at the relationship between the floors of a multi-storey building: it would be nonsense to say that the first and second floors are caused by the ground floor, even though they rest upon it, have some sort of relationship to it. Each is separate from the floor above and below it, and what goes on on each floor is not determined by what goes on below it. The first floor might be a shop, the second floor offices and the third floor living quarters. Althusser's term for describing this relation where there is a causal connection but not complete dependence is 'relative autonomy'. The political and ideological levels are neither completely dependent on the economic nor completely independent. If we take this building as a single enterprise, the office work which goes on on the second floor obviously depends upon the sort of trading that goes on in the shop but there are various ways in which it might be organised, and the work relationships there may develop in ways not influenced by the economic activity going on below. Similarly if the owners live on the third floor their standard of living and way of life has its limits set by the nature of the business they run but there are choices within these limits and the development of a marriage and family life has its own dynamics.

Althusser's next step away from crude Marxism is to argue that the causal processes are two-way: the political and ideological levels affect the economic. Returning to the example, decisions based on administrative criteria in the offices may have an effect on the trading in the shop – a 'streamlining of the management structure' for example, might lead to increased turnover. Similarly if the business is jointly owned and the marriage fails, the settlement between the partners might have an important effect on the nature of the business.

As you might expect from this perception of the structure of class society, Althusser argues that the study of history reveals periods when one level dominates over the other two but that this is never a permanent state of affairs. Thus it could be argued that 'the structure in dominance', as he calls it, in nineteenth-century capitalism was the economic, with the industrial bourgeoisie dominating not only economic but eventually political life, too. The power of the ideological level, mainly represented by the church, could be said to have dominated feudal society, while today a strong case could be made for seeing the structure in dominance in present-day Britain to be the political, via the power of the state and its penetration into so many aspects of life.

Althusser is also well known for a conceptual separation of the two elements by which the state exercises its power. He refers to organisations like the police, the army, the law and so on as constituting a *repressive state apparatus*. Alongside this political apparatus is an ideological one – the *ideological state apparatus* – made up of educational, media, religious and cultural institutions. Althusser's conception of a layered, interconnected structure is apparent here too; just as different structures in dominance prevail at different times in history, so different elements of a particular level will dominate at different times. Thus in modern society, education has taken over from religion as the principal ideological instrument of oppression; the work of Bowles and Gintis (1976) on the correspondence between the needs of capitalism and the function of education is Althusserian theory in practice.

## CONCLUSIONS

Despite the efforts of such schools of neo-Marxist thought, capitalism still seems under no threat. Indeed, living in the 1990s we now have to add the (for Marxists) calamitous events in Eastern Europe. Not only have communist regimes collapsed like cards, and not only has the Soviet Union self-destructed, but an ancient form of political ambition has emerged to replace communism in Eastern Europe – nationalism. Furthermore, the new post-communist regimes now settling old nationalist scores seem also to be rushing headlong to embrace capitalism, the free market and *laissez-faire* individualism.

None of this *necessarily* means that Marxist theory is a bad theory of capitalism, however. Just because it has been found wanting as a theory of political action does not mean it is therefore faulty as a theory of the political economy of capitalism. While events of the twentieth century may have brought into question Marx's version of the project of modernity, this does not mean that Marxist theory is failing to continue to provide us with the best set of analytical tools with which to make sense of modern capitalist societies. Here the questions are: 'Is the mode of production the defining characteristic of society? Is class always the central organising principle? Are ideas ultimately influenced by economic organisation?' It is against such conclusions that Marx's contemporary, Max Weber, presented his alternative analysis of modern capitalist society.

# CHAPTER FOUR

# *Max Weber*

As we have seen, functionalism and Marxism, while giving very different accounts of modern social life, are nonetheless similar types of theory. For both, the world is as it is because of the characteristics of the social structure; change occurs because of the dynamics of the system, and these theories of the system show how it works and how change takes place.

Of course, people living in different societies have their *own* theories of their worlds, but these mental states usually do not correspond with structural reality, and usually have no influence on the way the social world is. This is why functionalists talk of 'latent' and 'manifest' functions and why Marxists talk of 'false consciousness'. The idea that people should see how the world really is is unimportant in functionalism. While it is ultimately crucial for Marxism (other than in Althusserian Marxism), it only comes about when economic developments via the workings of the system encourage it, or when it is deliberately promoted by education. For functionalism all of the time, and for Marxism most of the time, then, mental states have no consequence for the structure of society. Weber's sociology is opposed to this kind of theory.

For Weber, the world is as it is because of social action. People do things because they *decide* to do so in order to achieve ends they desire. Having selected their goals, and taken account of the circumstances they find themselves in, they *choose* to act. Social structures are the *outcome* of such action; ways of living are the product of motivated choice. Existing action-created social circumstances exercise constraint as structural forces, of course; but action is nonetheless still *mental* in origin – *chosen* in the light of the actor's *perception* of these structural constraints. Understanding social, action-produced reality involves explaining *why* people make the choices they do. Sociological theories are not theories of social *systems*, which have their own dynamics, but of the meanings behind actions – they are theories of the theories of actors. Weber called the method by which this is done *Verstehen*. Because sociologists are human too, we can put ourselves in the place of others, appreciate the structural circumstances in which they find themselves, take account of their goals, and thereby *understand* their actions. This is what distinguishes a social science from a natural science. Daffodils don't *choose* to open their leaves and apples don't *decide* to fall from trees. Natural scientists therefore don't have to be like daffodils or apples to explain *their* behaviour.

Unlike most action sociology, however (see Chapter 6), Weber's interest in actors' theories, in motivated, goal-oriented action, does not mean that he is only interested in the small-scale, in the meaning of specific interaction between individuals. Like Marx, Weber is interested in the broad sweep of history and social change; in the words of Parkin (1982), for Weber, 'whole societies could be characterised by the typical forms of action to be contained within them'. But unlike Marx and Durkheim, who saw their task as uncovering *universal* tendencies in human social life, Weber rejects such a project. Weber reconstructs the meaning behind historical events producing social structures and formations, but at the same time sees all such historical configurations of circumstances as unique.

Weber argues that you can *compare* the structure of societies by understanding the reasons for the respective historical actions and events which have influenced their character, and by understanding the actions of actors living in them now, but that it is not possible to generalise about *all* societies or *all* social structures. To assist this kind of comparison, Weber argues that sociology should use as wide a range of concepts as possible.

## TYPES OF ACTION

Weber uses a classification of four types of action, differentiated in terms of the motives of actors:

| | |
|---|---|
| **Traditional action** | 'I do this because I've always done this.' |
| **Affective action** | 'I can't help doing this.' ('Everything I do, I do it for you.' Bryan Adams, 1991) |
| **Value-oriented action** | 'All I care about is this' or 'nothing matters except . . .' |
| **Goal-oriented, or rational action** | 'This is the most efficient way to achieve *this*', but '*this* is the most efficient way to achieve *that*', while 'I'll do *this* because I want *that*'. |

## TYPES OF INEQUALITY

Though, like Marx, Weber saw relations of inequality as central to social life, he rejects the Marxist notion that class inequality is always the most important. For him, comparative and historical analysis testifies that **status groups** – possessing certain amounts of prestige – and **parties** – possessing certain amounts of political influence – can be just as significant sources of advantage as **class** membership. Furthermore, Weber defined class not simply as the possession of productive property, as Marx did, but as the possession of all of the kinds of life-chances generated by 'market power' in a society – that is, in terms of the individual's capacity to solicit rewards for the sale of his or her skills in society's market-place.

## TYPES OF DOMINATION

Similarly, Weber rejects the Marxist notion that power is always tied to class membership. According to Parkin (1982) an interest in power and force suffuses his work: 'Domination . . . is one of the most important elements of social action . . . in most of the varieties of social action domination plays a considerable role . . . without exception every sphere of social action is profoundly influenced by structures of dominancy.'

Parkin (1982) shows how Weber's typology of power identifies different appeals for legitimacy by the powerful:

| *Type of domination* | *Grounds for claiming obedience* |
|---|---|
| **Traditional** | 'Obey me because this is what our people have always done.' |
| **Charismatic** | 'Obey me because I can transform your life.' |
| **Legal-rational** | 'Obey me because I am your lawfully appointed superior.' |

By developing his conceptual apparatus in this way, away from the sort of reliance on economic factors that characterises Marx's work, Weber has often been portrayed as engaging in a major attempt to refute the economic determinism of Marxism. Since he sees ideas and motives as the driving force in social life, he certainly wants to refute economic determinism; his sociology is quite clearly wholly antagonistic to the view that all social behaviour can be understood as being economically caused. However, as we have seen, while some of Marx's contemporaries who followed him were crudely economistic, it is not a charge that can be fairly levelled at Marx himself, as Weber in fact recognised in his comments on Marx's work. But there is another reason why it is wrong to see Weber's writings as a deliberate attempt to *disprove* Marx. This is because of the way he views the human activity of theorising.

## IDEAL TYPES AND SOCIOLOGICAL THEORISING

According to Weber, the most obvious truth about thinking is that no human being can possibly grasp the whole of reality he or she confronts – the 'meaningless infinity of the world process' as he describes it. Humans can only make sense of an aspect of reality – a selection from the infinite aggregate of events. Your theory represents your selection – your choice of what you think is worth looking at, and your choice of what you think explains these things. But this does not make your personal, selected, partial account objectively correct – objective truth is unavailable to a human theorist. As Weber (1978) puts it, 'all knowledge of cultural reality . . . is always knowledge from *particular points of view. . . .*' There can be no such thing as an 'absolutely "objective" scientific analysis of culture or . . . of "social phenomena" independent of special and "one-sided" viewpoints. . . . '

What we think exists depends upon what we think something's essence is. Thus, a functionalist might see a family as a system-integrating institution; a Marxist might see the same collection of people as a means of reproducing capitalism; while a feminist might see them as living lives which systematically oppress and subordinate the woman who is wife and mother. 'Seeing' therefore, is 'selecting'; 'seeing' is always theoretical.

Since seeing from a particular point of view is an inevitable part of being human, said Weber, we should not try to ignore the fact, but make it explicit in our accounts of the world. We should describe and explain reality by highlighting and emphasising our points of view to an extent which exaggerates the real world – by constructing *ideal-types* of reality, as Weber called them. To understand an aspect of social life, it is necessary to reduce it to what we think is its essence and then to highlight these features, so that others know exactly where we stand – what our point of view is. Our account of the world is 'ideal' not in a judgemental sense, but in a 'larger-than-life' sense; we paint our picture of the world – the aspects we consider significant or important to refer to

– in bold strokes, so others can be left in no doubt.

Unlike Marx and Durkheim then, Weber is not claiming to know the 'truth' about reality – only his version of it. Thus, in one of his most celebrated works (an account of the reasons for the emergence of modern capitalist society, and a portrayal of its principal features), Weber is not claiming that Marx is 'wrong' and he alone is 'right' in his theory. Weber regarded Marx's account as an ideal type and simply wanted to *add* his own account to Marx's, as an alternative, rather than claim to *refute* it.

However, it is easy to see why Weber's ideal-typical writings on modern society have been interpreted as an assault on Marxism, since he reverses the causal sequence Marx employs. Instead of seeing economic factors causing changes in ideas and beliefs, Weber explains the rise of modern capitalist society the other way round – particular ideas and beliefs emerge first, and thereby allow the establishment of capitalist production. Furthermore, the defining feature of capitalism for Weber is not, as it is for Marx, a mode of production, but an attitude, or a 'spirit' – a way of looking at things.

## RELIGION, CAPITALISM AND RATIONALISATION

Much of Weber's historical, comparative work is focused on the influence of religious beliefs on action. It is in this tradition that he sets out his account of the factors that encouraged the emergence of capitalism in those countries where it took root. This form of modern society, he argues, represents the institutionalisation of *rational* action above all else; whereas in other times and places other forms of action have prevailed, it is only in modern industrial capitalist societies that it has become routine for actors to act due to reasons of *efficiency* and *calculability*, rather than because of emotional or traditional reasons, or because of a single-minded dedication to an overriding goal. For Weber, modernity is best understood as the triumph of this way of thinking, this way of looking at the world, and this way of acting (though the last thing he wants to do is to join in the celebration). Modern capitalism is the end result of a *rationalisation process*, rooted in the historical influence of specific intellectual traditions. The emergence of this way of living and acting is, for Weber, 'the central problem in a universal history of civilization'; his investigation into this history is guided by the question of why it was, in non-Western countries, that 'neither scientific nor artistic nor political nor economic development followed the path of rationalisation which is unique to the West.'

In Weber's account, according to Bilton *et al.* (1987), the role of religious leaders in promoting differing kinds of ideas and orientations in different societies is crucial: 'For example, the Buddhist monk withdrew from all wordly activity in order to achieve a spiritual elevation, while the Confucian Mandarin engaged in administration on the basis of highly traditionalistic and non-scientific literary knowledge. Only in the west did a cultural orientation emerge which favoured rationalisation.'

The part of Weber's argument which has become most famous concerns the role of Puritan Protestantism, and particularly Calvinism, in this process. In *The Protestant Ethic and the Spirit of Capitalism* (1977) Weber outlines the affinity he sees between the kind of lives Calvinists were encouraged to lead by their religion, and the kind of behaviour and attitudes necessary for capitalism to work effectively. Weber stresses how, unlike in most religions, Calvinists are encouraged to concentrate on worldly work as the most virtuous activity and, at the same time, are exhorted to live ascetic – frugal, thrifty and austere – lives. Weber argues that this emphasis on the importance of industriousness and hard work, coupled with a demand for an ascetic lifestyle, is unique to Puritan religions, and that this combination of religious prescriptions gives capitalism the chance to take root. Calvinists believe they cannot prove to themselves and others that they have been called by God to salvation, as a predestined member of his Elect, unless they are successful and productive in their life's work; their belief is that the Lord will only let the worthy prosper. Their lives therefore become a dedication to efficiency and rationality, in order to maximise their productivity. But the symbols of their achievement, material riches accumulated through constant, ever-more-efficient labour, cannot be consumed in any profligate, ostentatious or self-indulgent fashion, since this would contradict the other Calvinist virtue of asceticism. Thus, although wealth accumulation is the symbol of virtuous and efficient hard work for Calvinists, the consumption of the fruits of this labour is denied the believer because of the need to live an ascetic life.

Here is the affinity with capitalism. Unlike other forms of economy, for capitalism to work, capital has to be accumulated; not to be consumed, but to be reinvested in the pursuit of ever-more-efficient, and profitable, techniques of production. The need is for the constant pursuit of rational means of production, by ploughing back the fruits of labour. The more wealth is made, and the more successful the capitalist enterprise is, the more resources are available to improve the efficiency of production. Work is therefore an end in itself; profit to be reinvested is virtuous, and brings its own reward.

Weber's account is clear. Only Puritanism expects of its followers a way of thinking and a way of living which matches the peculiar demands made on capitalist producers. Without a population dedicated to wordly work for its own sake, prepared to eschew as sinful any sign of extravagance, capitalism could not have got off the ground. The creation of such a world thus represents the perfect example of the Weberian view of the role of beliefs and action in social change; for Weber, capitalism is the child of a particular way of thinking and acting, not a mode of production spawned by economic forces. But, also for Weber, this child should have been strangled at birth, because it has grown into a monster.

Here is a different commentary on modernity from those of Weber's two main nineteenth-century peers. Weber's story is one of the role of specific intellectual traditions in specific historical circumstances, rather than the unravelling of inexorable and universally applicable laws of societal development, as are those of Durkheim and Marx. It is also the story of the social destruction of the human spirit by modernity. Durkheim and Marx constructed versions of a social theory which could specify the societal route to a future of progress and human emancipation. They both thought they had discovered the cure for social sickness and the recipe for societal, and thereby individual, health and happiness. For Durkheim, regulation through socialisation is guaranteed to prevent anomie; for Marx, historical materialism is the prescribed medicine for the eradication of the modern disease of alienation.

But Weber is no doctor of social life; he has no cure for rationalisation – for him, the scourge of modern society. For Weber, the pursuit of technical efficiency, whatever the (non-material) cost, is inevitable and irreversible in modern industrial capitalism, and while in bureaucratic administration it reaches its zenith, it also represents humanity's nadir. Weber tells us that the rise of this form of society means it is now wholly illusory to hope to build the sort of Utopia which the birth of modernity promised for so many thinkers. A world dominated by rationality – a world where efficiency, calculability and predictability are the dominant goals – means a world bereft of meaning, or of mystery, or of a concern with spiritual fulfilment. Weber tells us instead to resign ourselves to the 'iron cage of bureaucracy' and the 'polar night of icy darkness' which modernity has created. For Weber, the triumph of capitalism as a form of life signals the end of the line for progress; the train bearing the hopes for humanity's spiritual welfare has run into the buffers of terminal rationality.

## CONCLUSION

Much sociological theorising in the twentieth century can be seen to have its roots in the work of Durkheim, Marx and Weber. As we said earlier, until the 1960s (and particularly in the USA, through the dominance of functionalist analysis in the manner of Parsons and his followers), the influence of Durkheim outweighed that of his German counterparts. However, from the 1960s onwards this influence waned, particularly in Britain, and the work of modern followers of Marx and Weber (neo-Marxists and neo-Weberians) became much more significant.

But although much British neo-Marxist sociology since then has remained important – through the work of such as John Westergaard, Ralph Miliband and Peter Worsley, and the more recent contributions of writers like Stuart Hall – it is fair to say that neo-Weberian analysis has had a greater influence on the character of late-twentieth-century British sociology. During the 1960s and 1970s, neo-Weberians like David Lockwood, John Goldthorpe, John Rex and Ralf Dahrendorf all argued, following Weber, that though sociological analysis has to take proper account of relations of inequality, power and conflict, it should not be assumed that such phenomena can be reduced to economic factors. Furthermore, again in the Weberian tradition, such writers insisted that sociology also acknowledges the central importance of systems of ideas as instruments of continuity and change in social life. As we shall see, these twin Weberian interests, in structural relations *and* in the role of ideas, have remained important in the work of contemporary neo-Weberians like Gordon Marshall, Howard Newby and Mick Mann, and can be seen to have reached their greatest contemporary significance in the *structuration* theory of the leading British social theorist today – Anthony Giddens (see Chapter 10). Though Giddens has since developed his work in numerous ways beyond Weberian concerns, and though in very recent years, French philosophy and sociology have begun to reassert their influence on British sociology (see Chapter 7 and Chapter 10), it is nonetheless fair to say that over the past 20 years or so, the approach of Weber and his followers has had most influence over the practice of sociology in Britain.

In the field of *feminist* theorising, however, it is the ideas of Marx that have had most impact, and it is to feminist theories that we now turn.

# CHAPTER FIVE

# *Feminist theories*

For most of the time that sociological theorists debated the nature of modern society, a source of disadvantage experienced by half the world's population went unattended. The assumption was that the world as experienced by men was the same as that experienced by women. It was not until the political clamour of the 1960s and the renewed vigour of a women's movement, which originated at the turn of the century to secure the vote, that feminist theorising became established as an indispensable part of sociology. Sociological theories began to be constructed to explain the specific experiences of women and to point to, in good modernist fashion, the societal route to female emancipation and fulfilment. Just as the classic nineteenth-century theories were attempts to specify the possibility of progress via human theorising, so feminist theorists became engaged in a political project – to show how the acquisition of an understanding of the social conditions in which women live their lives opens up the opportunity to reconstruct their world, and thereby offer them the prospect of freedom.

## LIBERAL FEMINISM

Liberal feminism sees gender prejudice as a matter of individual ignorance, capable of being eradicated by the enforcement of anti-discrimination laws against the individuals concerned, and by the dispersal of non-sexist attitudes as a weapon in a war that can be won by re-education. The important sociological work of writers like Ann Oakley, in which the discrimination and disadvantage experienced by women is revealed through systematic empirical investigation, is often used in support of this kind of project.

Other feminist theorists take a more structural view of women's oppression however, locating it not in individual ignorance, but in *institutionalised* ways of living and thinking.

## MARXIST-FEMINISM

The first truly theoretical response to the need for a sociology of women was the claim that Marxism offered the best theoretical tool with which to excavate the foundations of their oppression. According to Marxist-feminists, women's subordination serves the needs of capitalism; it is in the economic relationships and ideas characteristic of the capitalist mode of production that we should look for the structures of disadvantage that unequally constrain women's lives in contrast to men's. The solution to the problem of women's oppression thus lies in the destruction of capitalism. Marxist-feminist approaches are of two main kinds – one more economistic than the other. The version of Marxist-feminism which focuses on the economic position of women in capitalist societies is characteristic of the work of writers like Veronica Beechey, Irene Bruegel and Wally Seecombe, among others. Their claim is that women's subordination is best explained by understanding the economic disadvantages they experience as a result of the requirements of capitalism. The following arguments have been advanced by contributors to the debate from this sort of perspective:

(1) Under capitalism, women live in families, as wives and mothers. In these families, women constitute a source of unpaid domestic labour, whose work is as vital for capitalism as that of the commodity producer in industry. Both by providing the domestic services necessary to sustain the male worker who is her husband, and by reproducing a new generation of workers through childcare, the woman as wife and mother is providing a crucial service for capitalism – free. It is therefore obviously far more profitable for capitalism to have women as unpaid domestic labourers than to have to pay male labourers the much higher wage they would need to purchase these domestic services in the marketplace.

(2) Also as a result of the normalcy of the nuclear family under capitalism, when women do enter the labour market, because they are seen as economically dependent on their husbands, they can be given low-paid, low-status and part-time work. Their work is seen as secondary and supplementary to that of their husbands', and so the rewards can be supplementary, too – married women's wages also need not be as high as those of single persons. In effect, married women are semi-proletarianised workers, economically more disadvantaged than the working class.

(3) Again, because of their economic dependence on their husbands, women as wives form a useful 'reserve army of labour', to be used in the labour market when required, but for whom permanent work is not a necessity. In effect, women are marginal workers, not just able

to be more poorly rewarded than males, but who can be brought in and out of the labour market as the need arises. The classic example of this was during the Second World War, when the absence of male workers meant that previously held prejudices against women had to be suspended so that crucial munitions work could be undertaken. Suddenly, women were needed in heavy industry, and all peacetime justifications for excluding them from such work were conveniently forgotten. Once the war was over, however, such ideologies and legitimations were trumpeted abroad once more.

(4) It is precisely these kinds of ideologies, justifying the world of women in capitalism, that more humanistically inclined Marxist-feminists stress, rather than economic factors. Writers like Michelle Barratt use the kind of approach advanced by Gramsci, arguing that the role of ideologies in extolling the virtues of family life, and of wifeliness and motherhood in domesticating women, are crucial in reproducing the features of the world from which they are disadvantaged. Barratt emphasises that the destruction of capitalist economic relations is a necessary, but not a sufficient, condition for the liberation of women. Also necessary is the transformation of ideas about sexuality, gender and parenthood, so that men and women are not ideologically coerced into living in one kind of marriage and in one kind of family.

Obvious problems present themselves with the Marxist-feminist account. If capitalism promotes women's subordination, why are women equally subordinated in non-capitalist societies? Though it is easy to see how the performance of unpaid domestic tasks clearly benefits capital, Marxist-feminism does not explain why it should be women who inevitably perform this labour. Why not men? Why not the old? *Radical feminism* attempts to explain the universality of women's oppression, and it does so by employing the concept of *patriarchy*. Patriarchy means the power of men over women; for radical feminists it is not an economic system that oppresses women – it is *men* who oppress women.

## RADICAL FEMINISM

For radical feminists, patriarchy is the key to understanding social structures. The *Red Stockings Manifesto* (1979) states that: 'Male supremacy is the oldest, most basic form of domination. All other forms of exploitation and oppression . . . are extensions of male supremacy . . . *All* men have oppressed women.'

So patriarchal relations are universal and elemental. Why should this be? Clearly, if there is one cause of patriarchy it must be found everywhere – as a ubiquitous part of the human condition. One of the first radical feminists, Kate Millett, argued that patriarchy is brought about by male control of ideas and culture. While this drew proper attention to institutionalised forms of belief oppressing women in ideologies at work, in education and in the family, Millet's *explanation* of these is rather tautological; in effect she tends to explain patriarchy by the exercise of patriarchy, which is hardly satisfactory. In other radical feminist work, three sorts of universals have been suggested – biological motherhood, marriage-based families and heterosexuality.

In another early radical feminist theory, that of Shulamith Firestone, the argument is that patriarchy is based on the biological fact that only females bear children. This approach claims that only when it becomes technologically possible to conceive and nurture children outside the womb will women be capable of being liberated. Then, gender differences will become irrelevant and the biological justification for trapping women in the role of mother in the family will disappear.

Other radical feminists argue that the universal phenomenon at the root of patriarchy is not biological motherhood, but the social institution of the family, based on marriage of one kind or another. For this version of radical feminism, marriage is what capitalism is for Marxist-feminists; according to Bouchier (1983), the 'real institutional source of exploitation'. Here we see a characteristic of radical feminist theorising that became established quite early on in its development – the notion that the 'personal is the political'. The exercise of power by men over women is found not just in the public structural and ideological features of work, education, the media, and so on. Just as important is patriarchy on the *personal* level, in the private world of intimate relations between men and women. As Mary Maynard (1989) puts it: 'Politics occur in families and between individuals when one person attempts to control or dominate another. It is in the personal and private sphere that women are particularly vulnerable to the power of men'. As Sylvia Walby (1990) says, from this point of view: 'The question of who does the housework, or who interrupts whom in conversation, is seen as part of the system of male domination.'

SEXUALITY

This emphasis on the politics of the private sphere has led some radical feminists to focus not so much on general interactions in families and marriages, as on the assumption of the normalcy of heterosexuality on which these universal institutions are based. Here the questions are,

'Why should "normal sex" be seen as "heterosexual sex"?', 'Why should "normal" heterosexual sex always involve the penetration of the woman's body by the man?', 'Why should the pursuit of vaginal orgasms (which benefit men) be seen as superior and necessary to sexual satisfaction than the pursuit of clitoral orgasms (for which men are not needed)?' The exposure of the vaginal orgasm as a physiological myth by Masters and Johnson in the 1960s added a new legitimacy to some radical feminist claims that the social construction of certain forms of sexuality as 'normal' and 'superior' to others is the universal device upon which patriarchy is founded. (Adrienne Rich calls this 'compulsory heterosexuality'.) From this point of view, the symbolism involved in 'normal' heterosexual (penetrative) sex is poignant; the act of penetration represents the colonisation of the woman's body and is, literally, a collusion with the enemy. Here sexual intercourse is the quintessential device by which men exercise dominance over women, for the argument is that once the body is controlled, the rest of a woman's life follows. (The radical feminist version of Richard Nixon's maxim, 'Once you've got them by the balls, their hearts and minds soon follow'?) As David Bouchier (1983) describes it:

> Once the myth of the vaginal orgasm was out of the way, it became possible to conceive a complete sexual revolution which would enable women to escape the sexual domination of men. If women did not need men, and could make an unrestricted choice of heterosexual, bisexual, lesbian or celibate life-styles, the resulting liberation of sexual behaviour would break the hold of the monogamous family, the source of patriarchal power.

In practice, this goal of the transformation of women's sexuality as the route to the destruction of patriarchy has led many radical feminists to argue that only lesbian sexuality allows women the freedom to express their emotional selves – a solution known as 'separatism'.

VIOLENCE

The emphasis on heterosexuality as the basis of patriarchy has led radical feminist theorists to explore the links between sexual hegemony and violence against women. The work of Susan Brownmiller, Adrienne Rich and Andrea Dworkin, among others, is notable here. In societies like that of Great Britain, a significant element in the social construction of heterosexuality is the public presentation of women as compliant and accommodating, available playthings for men to make use of in the pursuit of their sexual gratification. Hardly any thought is needed to see that such images abound in advertising, the media and along the top shelves of countless newsagents. The radical feminist point here is that if women are presented in this sexually available way, with the explicit invitation to be used by men, sexual harassment, assault or rape should not be seen as surprising. These are merely more violent expressions of 'normal' sexual relations between men and women. To see such acts as evidence of depravity or sickness is to miss the point about the definition of what sex should be about from which they spring.

For many radical feminists the woman's world is suffused with the prospect of real or potential violence by men, violence endorsed by the symbolic violence of heterosexual sex, and promoted by advertising and pornography. If some men structure some aspects of their lives because of the threat of physical assault – avoiding certain places at night, or refusing to drink in 'rough' pubs – then radical feminism points at the much more routine problems faced by women. According to Elizabeth Stanko (1985):

> Women know about the unpredictability of men's physical and sexual intimidation. We plan our lives around it: finding the right street to walk down when coming home, cooking the eggs the way the husband likes them, and avoiding office parties are examples of strategies designed to avoid male sexual and physical intimidation and violence.

## DUAL-SYSTEMS THEORIES

Dual-systems theories involve a fusion of Marxist-feminist and radical feminist ideas, recognising the impact of both capitalism and patriarchy as instruments of women's oppression. Most contributions so far tend to use a version of patriarchy rooted in marriage and the family, rather than in sexuality and violence.

Christine Delphy, who calls her theory *materialist feminism*, employs Marxist methods and concepts, but eschews a straightforward Marxist approach. According to Delphy there are two class-based modes of production in capitalist society, the industrial and the domestic. The industrial mode of production involves the exploitation of the proletariat by the bourgeoisie, while the domestic mode features the patriarchal exploitation of women by men. The usual view of the family, as a unit in which the class membership of the members is determined by the economic status of the husband, is thus supplemented by a view of the family as an arena in which representatives of two other classes co-exist and in which class exploitation also occurs of a kind that parallels the industrial mode. Thus, while working men are exploited in the industrial mode, they become the exploiters in the domestic mode; single women are exploited in the industrial mode, but most women's exploitation is experienced in the domestic mode because most women get married and become domestic workers.

Delphy's main effort is to explain the patriarchal exploitation of women. She is far less concerned with the impact of capitalism. Other dual-systems theorists have the balance of interests much more equal.

Zillah Eisenstein sees capitalism and patriarchy as being so intimately connected that they actually form one system, which she calls *capitalist patriarchy*. Their interconnection is so profound that changes in one part of the system cause changes in the other. Thus, for example, an increase in women working in the labour market because of the needs of capital would necessarily cause pressure for political change, because of the impact of this on women's role as domestic labourers.

In *The Unhappy Marriage of Capitalism and Feminism*, Heidi Hartmann also insists on the need to see women as oppressed by both men and capitalism, but sees these features as constituting separate, though connected, systems of oppression. Thus, women are exploited by men both in the labour market – men have the better rewarded jobs – and in the household – women do more domestic labour than men, even if they are also wage-earners. Patriarchy came into being prior to capitalism through marriage and family relations, and with the development of capitalist relations of production men have, as it were, 'done a deal' with capitalism to secure the kind of advantages over women in this new sphere of waged work which they had previously enjoyed in the domestic sphere. Thus the Labour movement in Great Britain has mainly promoted the interests of men, not women. Both parties benefit from women's exploitation at home and in work. Capitalism benefits from women's economic dependence on men because this ensures their availability for insecure, low-paid employment, and men benefit because they get the better jobs and have domestic services provided for them.

Juliet Mitchell also sees capitalism and patriarchy constituting two separate but related sources of oppression for women, but believes patriarchy is rooted in the unconscious rather than in the household. Mitchell's approach is rather controversial in feminist circles because she sees the universality of patriarchy not as a consequence of ubiquitous domestic or sexual relations in human life, but as part of the process of the formation of the female psyche. She uses Freudian ideas to claim that women develop a sense of self which allows their domination by men, but that this process takes place at an unconscious level, rather than by overt ideological manipulation. This can make its alteration a matter for psychoanalysis rather than political action.

## ANTI-ESSENTIALISM

One of the commonest objections to all these Marxist-feminist and radical feminist approaches is that they are based on the assumption that all women experience the world in the same way – that women can be classed together and theorised about en masse, as if there is an *essence* to *all* women's lives. Black feminists in particular object to this, arguing that it commits the same kind of error as gender-blind, male-oriented sociological theorising. This is also the point of departure for *post-structuralist feminists* (see pp. 170–1).

Black feminists point out that while gender may be the main source of oppression experienced by White, middle-class women, Black women are typically oppressed by their race and class as well. This means that White feminist theorising often misses the mark so far as Black women's lives are concerned. What is a source of oppression for White women may be a source of liberation for Blacks; whereas the family can be the principal instrument of subordination for White women, it can be a haven from a racist outside world for Blacks. White women are often the racist oppressors, which hardly equates with the concept of 'sisterhood' – women's solidarity. When White women talk of the need to expand opportunities for women to work in the labour market in order to liberate themselves from the stranglehold of domesticity, they do not usually mean the kind of work many Black women are *forced* to do, since most Black women are working class. Again, when White women clamour for the 'right to choose' – the right to have abortions – this hardly makes sense to some Third World Black women, who live in societies characterised by enforced terminations and sterilisations and the use of drugs like Depo-Provera. For them, it is the right to *keep* their fertility that is at stake. Finally, the preoccupation with sexuality among some White feminists is profoundly irrelevant for many women in the Third World, where poverty and starvation and a lack of education are ubiquitous; there is not much point concentrating your energies on orgasms if you have no food, shelter or medicine.

# CHAPTER SIX

# *Interpretive sociology: action theories*

## SYMBOLIC INTERACTIONISM

Symbolic interactionism (SI) is the name given to one of the best-known action theories. It is with symbolic interactionism that the phrases, 'definition of the situation', 'reality is in the eye of the beholder' and, 'if men define situations as real, they are real in their consequences' are most usually associated.

Though rather cumbersome, the name given to this perspective does clearly indicate the kinds of human activity which its proponents consider essential to concentrate on in order to understand social life. According to SI theorists, social life literally is the 'interaction of humans via the use of *symbols*'. That is, they are interested in:

(a) the way in which humans employ symbols of what they mean in order to communicate with one another (an orthodox interpretive interest);

(b) the effects that the interpretations of these symbols have on the behaviour of parties during a social interaction.

In our earlier discussion of action theory, we emphasised how the behaviour of human beings must essentially be the product of how they interpret the world around them. It is not behaviour which is *learnt* or *determined*, as structural theories suggest. Rather, it is *chosen* as appropriate behaviour in the light of how people *define* the situations they encounter – what they take social settings to *mean*.

But a question we did not consider earlier is this. How far does this process of interpretation, which, according to action theorists, is always the origin of behaviour, affect *other* people involved in these meaningful encounters? This is clearly important. As we said in Chapter 1, most of the situations in which we find ourselves are inevitably *social* situations – they involve *other* people doing things. Nearly every time we interpret meaning in order to decide how to act we are interpreting the actions of other human beings.

One of the principal interests of SI has been to consider this very question – the effects of interpretation *on the person whose actions are being interpreted*.

SI stresses that *interaction* is a two-way interpretive process. We must not only understand that someone's action is a product of how *they* have interpreted the behaviour of someone else, but that this interpretation will have an impact on the actor whose behaviour has been interpreted in certain ways too. One of the major contributions of symbolic interactionism to action theory has been to elaborate and explain the different kinds of effects which the interpretations of others can have on the social identities of the individuals who are the objects of these interpretations.

## The construction of self-image

The most common effect is that we use the interpretations of others – what they take our behaviour to mean – as evidence of who we think we are. That is, our self-image is a product of the way others think of us – in effect, I am what I think you think I am.

For SI this is largely what socialisation means. It is not, as structural theorists argue, a process whereby given external, cultural rules are generally internalised by people. It is an outcome of the interpretive process – the allocation of meaning between people – that for action theorists is at the root of all social interaction. Our personalities are constructed by means of this interpreting process as follows.

During the course of our lives, we encounter a number of people, all of whom take our behaviour towards them to symbolise something about our selves. They interpret our behaviour in the light of the evidence they are provided with. They then act towards us in the light of this interpretation, indicating via the symbolic means available to them what kind of person they have decided we are. The image we have of ourselves is crucially influenced by the reactions of individuals we come into contact with. We cannot ignore what kind of person others are telling us we are; the image of our 'self' is seriously affected, if not created, by the image others have of us.

Take, for example, the relationship between a primary school teacher and his/her class. Being human, the teacher cannot help but make judgements about the children in the class, particularly about their ability. Equally, according to SI, since the children are human too, their view of themselves and their abilities will be influenced by the judgement of the teacher. So the little boy who sits attentively at the front of the class, behaves well and is keen and conscientious, is likely to be thought of as 'intelligent' or 'able'. In contrast, the girl who sits at the back of the class, inattentive and lazy, is less favourably interpreted.

SI argues that often what matters is not whether the interpretations are correct, but the impact they can have on their recipients. In this case, even though the children are in fact of the same ability, the teacher has decided they are not, and as a result treats them differently. The little boy is encouraged to work, whereas the little girl is merely admonished for misbehaviour and kept under control.

These different reactions of the teacher influence the way the children see themselves. Sustained by the support and encouragement of the teacher, the little boy works hard and fulfills his potential. Persuaded by the teacher that she has little academic ability, the girl concentrates on misbehaving. The teacher's judgements are thus confirmed; the prophecy about the children's abilities comes true. The justice of the interpretations matters less than the consequences of their application, particularly in the way the recipients are encouraged to see themselves.

The fortuity of the outcome of this process of interaction between interpreter and interpreted is plain to see. Our 'self' – the person we become – depends upon the *particular* people we happen to encounter in our journey through life. *Other* parents, friends, acquaintances, and workmates could make us into very different people. In our example, a different teacher might have encouraged both children equally, with much more positive consequences for the little girl's self-image.

But the influence of the interpretations of others is only one half of the process of interaction emphasised by SI. Far from human personality being simply the passive construction of others, SI stresses the *active* role which humans play in the creation of their social selves. According to SI, since we soon come to learn that others will interpret our behaviour, our *own* interpretive abilities allow us to manipulate these interpretations to suit our vision of ourselves. We use our capacity to be *self-reflexive* in order to present the person we wish others to think we are. We play roles in a *creative way* to elicit from others the responses we desire. In effect, we manage, or orchestrate, the responses of others by presenting the image of our *self* that we wish them to hold. We become actors on the stage of life, writing our own lines.

The SI theorist most commonly associated with this emphasis on creative role-playing is Erving Goffman. In a book called *The Presentation of Self in Everyday Life* (1969), Goffman outlines his conception of social life as a stage upon which humans play themselves, and explains the social props that are pressed into service to present these selves to others.

According to Goffman, very few human attributes, possessions or activities are not used in this theatrical way. The clothes we wear, the house we live in, the way we furnish it, the way we walk and talk, the work we do, and the way in which we spend our leisure time – everything that is public about ourselves can, and is, used to tell others what kind of person we are. We thus 'manage' the information we provide for others. We control our dress, appearance and habits to encourage others to see us as the people we claim to be.

For Goffman and his fellow interactionists, socialisation is usually about the triumph of the creative capacities of the individual over the reactions of others. Not all action theorists agree, however. *Labelling theory* is a perspective which has grown out of symbolic interactionism. Labelling theory is less interested in the ways in which people are able to influence others' interpretations of themselves than in the kinds of interaction where no such opportunities exist. Labelling theorists are mainly interested in the fact that sometimes people are victims, often helpless, of the interpretations, or *labels*, of others to such an extent that their social identities *can* be imposed upon them, even against their will.

Why should this happen? Why should we find ourselves in social situations where we *cannot* manipulate the interpretations of others?

## LABELLING THEORY: THE PERSON AS VICTIM

*Labels which contradict the self-image*

Sometimes we are in no position to protest against misinterpretation, because we are dead. For example, as already briefly discussed in Chapter 1, a verdict of suicide depends on the interpretations of a range of people – kin, friends, police officers and, in particular, coroners. Though bodies often indicate the truth, everything eventually depends on others' interpretations. As we shall see in Chapter 9, those charged with deciding cause of death sometimes pay little heed to the efforts of suicides to manipulate the label they desired.

Sometimes we *can* protest against a wrong label, but this cuts no ice with our interpreters. For example, it is the public labelling of a person as a shoplifter in court, and later on in the local press, that will be the evidence others will go on, not our protestations of innocence.

In any case, sometimes these protestations are merely seen as confirmation of the appropriateness of the label. For example, if you are diagnosed as being mentally ill even though you consider yourself perfectly sane, it is likely that you will make a considerable fuss about the prospect of being carted off to a mental hospital. Normal though this reaction may be from your point of view, the danger is that your angry or excitable behaviour will be seen by others as confirmation that you are unbalanced. 'After all, no *normal* person would get into that state.' Finally, even if we rise above the interpretations of others and attempt to *ignore* what we consider a wrong label and act normally, it is perfectly possible that this can simply serve to confirm its justice to others. For example, when you are diagnosed as mentally ill, if you *don't* make a fuss and act as normally as possible in order to prove your sanity, this too may simply be interpreted as confirmation of your diagnosed condition. 'After all, no *normal* person would just *sit* there like that.'

Goffman's classic interactionist account of hoarding behaviour among mental patients in *Asylums* (1968), is a very good example of the confirmatory character of 'normal' behaviour once the 'abnormal' label has been applied. Hoarding is a very common feature of the behaviour of patients in mental hospitals. All sorts of apparently useless and trivial objects – like pieces of string and toilet paper – are constantly in the possession of many of the inmates, who steadfastly refuse to let them out of their sight for a moment. The usual interpretation of this behaviour serves to confirm the label attached to the patient. It is argued that it is obviously abnormal to have such worthless items permanently about one's person and such hoarding can only be a reflection of considerable and deep-seated anxieties and insecurities.

Goffman disputes this analysis, arguing that it only seems appropriate from the standpoint of life *outside* the mental hospital, where such 'useless' items are always available. Inside the institution, however, where, for the inmate, they are much more difficult to come by, it makes very good sense to look after them very carefully. Furthermore, since mental hospital patients tend to lack both privacy and storage facilities, an obvious place to keep them secure is about one's person.

All of these examples, then, are of victims of misinterpretations whose contradictory accounts either cannot be heard or will not be listened to.

Labelling theory argues that sometimes the process of labelling can be so overwhelming that even the victims of misinterpretation cannot resist its impact. Faced with a persistently applied label, the self-image of the labelled person crumbles. He or she comes to see himself or herself anew, embracing the alternative image others have applied.

As in the earlier effects of labelling, the correctness, or 'truth', of the label has little to do with the power of its impact. Right or wrong in *fact*, its application and the reactions of others to its existence *make* it true. Once again, the prophecy is fulfilled, but in this case it becomes the reality for both the beholder *and* the beheld.

*The alteration of self-image*

The identification of this process has been a feature of the application of labelling theory to deviance – the area where it has probably been most influential. One of its most significant contributions to the study of deviant behaviour has been to show that the identification of deviance is a product of the interpretation of a particular individual in a particular social setting (as is all labelling). It has also shown that the reactions of others to a labelled deviant are often so severe that they produce a dramatic alteration in an already established self-image.

## LEMERT AND PARANOIA

Edwin Lemert's famous account of the social construction of paranoia demonstrates both these aspects of labelling very clearly. Paranoia is a mental condition in which the sufferer imagines he or she is being persecuted by a conspiracy. However, as Lemert (1967) points out, if paranoia is suspected in somebody then such a conspiracy actually does come into being. The 'ill' person is observed secretly. Since mentally disturbed people do not know what is good for them, and can act irrationally, attempts to organise treatment will also be clandestine; visits to doctors and psychiatric hospitals will be organised behind the patient's back. Any suspicion on the part of the suspected paranoid that this sort of thing is going on will, naturally enough, lead him or her to complain about it. Normal though such resentment may be from the labelled person's standpoint, in the eyes of its applicators this will merely serve to confirm the justice of the label. Clearly, here *is* someone who believes he or she is being conspired against by others. The fact that this is actually what *is* happening won't defer the labellers' from having their judgement confirmed.

Such confirmation may lead to a stay in a mental hospital for treatment. It is at this stage in the construction of paranoia that persons so labelled experience the most sustained pressure on their self-images. Lemert argues that however certain they are of their sanity prior to institutionalisation, organisational confirmation of the 'insane' label, particularly by means of deliberate attempts to change behaviour, will finally sink without trace inmates' previously held self-images. The suspicion grows that maybe everyone else was right all along and that they were too ill to appreciate their condition. After all, why else would they be in hospital?

For the labellers of such people, particularly the psychiatric staff, this stage of self-image alteration – an acknowledgement of the need for treatment – is the first major step en route to a cure. The fact that it might simply be the *last* stage in the *social* construction of a mental condition, which began not with any real illness, but with an initial labelling by others is, of course, not considered.

The impact which *organisational* labelling is designed to have on the construction of social personality and, particularly, on the creation of a new self-image, has been powerfully articulated by Goffman.

## GOFFMAN AND INSTITUTIONALISATION

According to Goffman, the official treatment of many kinds of deviant behaviour in organisations set up for the purpose, is, as in the case of mental illness, a quite self-conscious attempt to alter the deviant's self-image, so that he or she may become more amenable to 'cure'. In a celebrated account of what he calls *'total institutions'* (*Asylums*, 1986) Goffman advances the view that establishments like prisons, concentration camps and mental hospitals, where labelled deviants are completely incarcerated over considerable periods, are essentially agencies of resocialisation. Though his argument is not confined to the treatment of deviants (he claims that the same principles underpin the rigorous training undergone by, for example, soldiers and the members of some religious orders) the *involuntary* nature of the deviants' membership of such institutions makes any successful alteration to their self-images particularly noteworthy.

Goffman (1968) defines total institutions as: 'places of residence and work where a large number of like-situated individuals cut off from the wider society for an appreciable period of time, together lead an enforced, formally administered round of life.' He argues that in such establishments, the organisation of life is deliberately designed to strip the inmate of his or her self-image and replace it with one more acceptable to the ethos of the institution. He calls this process *'institutionalisation'*.

For example, he says, admission procedures are often designed to remove all visible symbols of the inmate's former self and replace them with indications of the new person he or she is to be trained to be. Thus, names are often replaced by numbers (as in prisons, concentration camps and military establishments), or by new names (as in religious orders). The inmate's physical appearance is sometimes altered as visibly as possible; clothing is often removed on entry and replaced with institutional uniforms, and hair is cut in a severe fashion. Since the acquisition of possessions may be frowned upon and made difficult, all or most personal property is often confiscated on entry. Personal space may be denied, even for the most private of activities.

In these ways, and in others, says Goffman, inmates are stripped of the props by which they retained a sense of their former selves and were able to communicate this to others.

Furthermore, attempts to alter the self-image of the inmate can be reinforced by its *debasement*, in ritual and other ways – a process Goffman calls the *'mortification of the self'*. For example, new inmates may have to undergo humiliation upon entry, such as strip-searching (in prison) or ritual ablution (in mental hospital). During their incarceration inmates are often obliged to behave in the most obsequious and obedient manner towards the institution's staff, sometimes in the face of provocation. Such degradations, often in public, are designed, argues Goffman, to mortify the former self of the inmate, to render it soiled and thereafter unusable, and to encourage its replacement by a new identity, more suitable to meet the demands of the institution.

Though labelling theorists would normally expect such processes to prove irresistible to their recipients, Goffman is true to his interactionist principles. Believing that social identities are not just imposed on people but are created and recreated as a two-way interpretive process, Goffman stresses not only the impact of institutionalisation but the capacity of inmates to resist or adjust to the processes to which they are subjected to a greater or lesser degree. He talks of those who do become 'colonised', or institutionalised, preferring life in the institution to life outside, or of those who become 'converted', acquiescing to the staff's view of the model inmate and acting out the role to the limit. He also talks of inmates who protect their selves by withdrawing from interaction with others, or who do so by actively rebelling against the institution, as well as of those (the majority, in Goffman's view) who 'play it cool' – who stay out of trouble and maintain their self-image by playing whatever reactive role circumstances demand.

LABELLING RELATIONS AS POWER RELATIONS

If some labelling involves *victimisation* of the kind we have been discussing, then labelling theory argues that we have to ask a further, final question – where do these victims come from? For example, why do some people come to be labelled as mentally ill and not others? Why do *certain* children come to be labelled as uneducable, and not others?

For labelling theorists the answer lies not in any reality of different mental conditions or levels of intelligence. Rather, it lies in the origin of the *perception* of these attributes by others. The focus is on the reasons for these kinds of labels being attached to *certain kinds of people*, rather than on any characteristics the victims of these labels may or may not possess. The interesting question is therefore not 'How did these people *get* like this?' but 'Why did *these* people come to be labelled like this, and not others?', or 'Why are *these* people the victims of such labels and not other people?'

The usual labelling theory answer to these questions is that the application of such labels is ultimately about the exercise of *power*. According to labelling theory the most damaging labels in social life – those of *deviant* – usually become attached to the most helpless and least powerful members of society – those least capable of fighting back and resisting the process. This analysis of deviant labelling as a reflection of the exercise of power is described by Howard Becker, one of its leading exponents, as a process where the '*underdogs*' in a society become victims of its '*overdogs*'.

This is a feature of labelling approaches to deviant behaviour in general; deviants are generally seen as victims, not as wrongdoers. It is particularly evident in the typical labelling analysis of *crime*. Crime is seen exclusively as a product of labelling, and of the all-pervading impact that the allocation of such a label can have. Labelling theory sees the relationship between labellers and labelled in this area of social life as essentially one of power. Quite contrary to the conventional view, then, victims are the underdogs who are made into criminals, whereas wrongdoers are the more powerful overdogs who impel the powerless down a never-ending spiral of criminal deviance.

## LABELLING THEORY AND CRIME

Labelling theorists argue that there are two fundamental questions which have to be asked about crime:
(1) Why do some human activities come to be made illegal and not others?
(2) Why do some people become criminals and not others?

According to labelling theory, the answers to both these questions reflect the distribution of power in society. Not only are the powerful able to designate those acts which are illegal in a society, they are also able to influence who gets labelled as a criminal.

*Laws*

Labelling theory argues that although we might like to think that laws are somehow God-given or quite definitely in *everyone's* best interest, things are not quite as cosy as this. They stress that we have to recognise that the construction of legal rules is a *political* act. The decision that *this* action should be allowed, whereas another should not, is made by those humans who have the power to decide. Furthermore, 'the powerful' in this regard does not simply mean the *actual* law-makers, but also individuals or groups who are able to *influence* the law-makers – those people in a society whom Becker calls its 'moral entrepreneurs'.

Because of the relationship between power and the construction of legal rules, it is not surprising, say labelling theorists, that the acts that are not *illegal* in a society tend to be the acts in which the powerful engage. So, although it is perfectly possible to imagine a society in which it is illegal to inherit wealth, or profit from rent, or exploit Black labour in South African mines, or avoid paying taxes, yet *legal* to smoke marijuana, make homosexual advances in public, and engage in 'adult' activity at a much younger age than 18, this is not how things are. Laws reflect the distribution of power in that the less powerful are more likely to engage in those activities which the laws prohibit.

You might consider this a rather far-fetched view. After all, what about laws prohibiting tax evasion, the placement of contracts by public officials in return for reward, company fraud, or the monopolisation of production? Labelling theory grants that of course there are some laws which particularly affect the activities of, say, the wealthy, but it argues that these tend to be the laws which are *least* strenuously enforced. And even if they are vigorously enforced they tend to be the laws least likely to furnish a successful prosecution, because of the resources available to the powerful to defend themselves.

In effect then, the SI position is that the role of power in the construction of crime is not just restricted to the *definition* of illegal acts, but influences the investigation of crime too. And nowhere is this latter influence more apparent than in the selection of the individual criminal to prosecute – in the labelling of a particular person's actions as illegal.

*Law-breaking*

Why should some people be labelled as criminals and not others? The obvious answer to this is that only some people choose to commit crime. From this point of view, the job of any explanation of criminality – sociological, psychological or biological – is to discover what it is about these kinds of people that led them down the criminal path.

For labelling theory, however, things are not as straightforward as this, primarily because such an analysis ignores the huge discrepancy between the number of crimes committed and the number of criminals convicted.

Research demonstrates without doubt that the incidence of criminal activity bears little relation to the number of crimes known to the police (the C.K.P. index), and even less to the number of crimes for which the police get a conviction (the 'clear-up' rate).

The first national piece of research into both recorded and unrecorded crime in Britain, the first British Crime Survey (March 1983), demonstrated this clearly. Eleven thousand households were interviewed in order to identify the crimes they had suffered and the results compared with those on the C.K.P. index. The survey shows that five times as many violent crimes and four times as many property crimes are committed as those reported to the police. The degree to which the official statistics underplay the real level of crime depends on the particular category of crime. Almost all cars which are stolen are reported. It is the only way owners can receive compensation from insurance companies. Probably for the same reason (because more private property is now insured than before), the number of burglaries reported has increased; the survey suggests that one out of two is now reported. But other property crimes have much lower reporting rates. For example, only 13 per cent of acts of vandalism are reported, and it is estimated that probably only 1 per cent of all shoplifting offences are reported. Why should crimes be so under-reported?

Many crimes, such as vandalism, are not reported because of their petty nature. Yet even many violent crimes go unreported – only about 20 per cent of all woundings, sexual attacks and robberies are reported, for example. The main reason for this low rate seems to be the young age of many of the victims and their lack of faith either in the way the police will handle the complaint, or in the capacity of the police to solve the crime.

Earlier studies have shown that even when crimes are reported to the police they are not always recorded. The reasons for this include overwork, doubts about the validity of the allegations, and the temptation to improve the clear-up rates by not including insoluble crimes.

As well as such *victim surveys, self-report studies* also illustrate the wide gap between the commission of crime and the C.K.P. index and the even wider gap between commission and clear-up. Such studies ask people to volunteer their past illegal actions under a guarantee of absolute confidentiality. They reveal that anything between 50 per cent and 90 per cent of people admit some kind of illegal behaviour which could result in a court appearance if detected. Even more significant, they also indicate that criminal activity is distributed across all sections of society. They show that crimes are just as likely to be committed by the middle class as the working class, and they certainly demonstrate the error of assuming that crime is more likely to be concentrated in the lower strata of the class structure.

Yet this is precisely what the official conviction statistics – of crimes cleared up by the police – *do* indicate. The overwhelming impression from these figures is that crime is mainly committed by young, urban working-class males.

Why should this be? If, as self-report studies indicate, crime is *committed* by no particular kind of person, why do only certain kinds of people get *caught?*

The labelling theory answer, of course, is that only certain kinds of people are likely to be *labelled* as criminal. Being human, police can only take action against acts and people they *perceive* as breaking the law. *That* is why certain kinds of people become criminals. It is not because they are the only people who have committed crimes. Indeed it is not even because they necessarily *have* committed any crime at all. It is simply because they have been *interpreted* as having done so.

Why is there such a distinctive pattern to these interpretations? Labelling theorists argue that the perceptions of the police inevitably emanate from the stereotypes of criminals with which they and other agents of law enforcement operate.

Why stereotypes should prevail in law enforcement is clear enough. If, as self-report studies show, criminal activity is distributed equally throughout any population, then whatever stereotype of the 'typical criminal' you choose to operate, your judgement is going to be vindicated. But the important question is: why have some *stereotypes* come to prevail in the pursuit of crime, and not others?

According to labelling theory, we need look no further for our answer than at the distribution of power in society. In the same way that the powerful are able to influence the designation of certain acts as illegal rather than others, they are also able to encourage certain *perceptions of the criminal* – advantageous to themselves – to prevail. So although the official conviction statistics tell us very little about the actual distribution of crime in society, they do tell us much about the kinds of people policemen and other law enforcers are most likely to label as criminal. In turn, this tells us about the kinds of influences on stereotypes employed in law enforcement that the powerful have been able to bring to bear. The picture painted by the conviction statistics makes this clear. The chances of matching up to the stereotypes typically employed in law enforcement decrease as a person moves up the social hierarchy.

According to Bilton *et al.* (1987) criminal labels await the least advantaged members of society because they are powerless:

> We should not be surprised to find blacks and working-class people over-represented in the official statistics of crime, since they and their behaviour are more likely to fit law-enforcement agencies' perceptions of 'criminals' and 'crime', and they are less likely to be able to mobilise the material and social resources necessary to convince others that 'they're not like that'.

Of course, once the powerless receive their labels, the self-fulfilling prophecy just referred to will come into effect. The successful application of the stereotype will mean that its validity is confirmed for its users and it can be employed with even *more* conviction in the future. The process of criminal labelling thus *increases* the chances of the least powerful becoming criminals and *decreases* the chances of the most powerful. In this way, inequalities of power in society are cemented by the process of law enforcement. Furthermore, once the stereotype is applied and the label attached, the existence of the label promotes the usual self-fulfilling prophecy so far as any particular individual actor is concerned. Others react to the label in such a way that makes future 'normal' activity very difficult. Because of a conviction, other people may ostracise the labelled person or treat him or her with suspicion. Occupational opportunities may also become unavailable, and so on. The *stigma* of being branded a criminal overwhelms all other attributes; something someone is supposed to have *done* becomes what he or she *is*. Because of the reactions of others to the stigma of the label, the labelled person – whether guilty or innocent in *fact* – is, according to labelling theory, often impelled into pursuing the 'career' of a criminal, simply because all other normal options are closed down.

Obviously, this process of being forced into a deviant career by the reactions of others – known as *deviance amplification* – is not as immediately problematic for the self as, say, the misinterpretation of mental illness. After all, one usually knows whether one *was* guilty of an offence or not. Nevertheless, it can still mean that the labelled person's self-image is in danger of alteration, especially if the opportunities for a 'normal' existence are sufficiently restricted. Lacking any choice, labelled persons come to see themselves as the person they have been forced to become.

In an area such as crime, therefore, structural and action assumptions meet head on. Pursuing the external determinants of any social activity located in the social structure, the structural theorist looks for the reasons why, as the conviction statistics show, certain kinds of people come to commit criminal acts and some not. Armed with conviction statistics, which feature the urban working-class male above all other categories of person, those giving structural explanations of crime attempt to identify the reasons why a person in this sort of structural location is impelled to commit crime more often than other kinds of person.

One of the most popular explanations of this phenomenon is known as *sub-cultural theory*. Here crime is explained as the product of cultural or normative influences. The young working-class male, more often than any other kind of person, finds himself in a cultural setting where criminal activity is normal, and where conformity to such norms via socialisation gives rise to law-breaking. The sociological task is therefore to identify those cultural features that promote crime in this kind of social world, and not in others.

As in the case of all structural explanations then, the emphasis is on identifying the origins of the *external* social forces whose existence is manifested in the behaviour of individuals.

In contrast, labelling theory's approach to crime features the opposed action theory assumptions about social behaviour. Armed with *their* evidence – that crime is much more widespread among all social groups than the *conviction* rates show – labelling theorists are interested not in why young working-class males *commit* crimes more often than other people, but why they are more likely to be *labelled* as criminals than others. The interesting questions here, therefore, concern the reasons for their behaviour being interpreted as criminal, while that of other people is not. The labelling perspective focuses on the social construction of the reality of crime by the members of a society themselves, rather than on the determining influence on behaviour of a structural reality outside these members.

Yet, as the study of crime also shows, the structural and SI emphases are not as mutually exclusive as they might at first appear. The reason is that SI does not completely embrace an action theory approach to social life. We can see this in two aspects of its explanation of crime.

First, the idea of 'stereotypes' in the application of criminal labels refers to generally held views among those whose job it is to enforce the law. Since such generally held views will, for example, be encountered and embraced and therefore perpetuated by new recruits, this is clearly much closer to the structural view of socialisation into pre-existing normative definitions than pure action theory allows.

Second, the idea that powerful groups influence both the construction of laws, and the stereotypes of the criminal, is quite close to an orthodox structural perspective. For such a process to take place, particular groups must have the power to exercise influence, and others must lack the resources to resist. This vision of social life as being crucially influenced by the unequal distribution of advantage between groups is, of course, a conventional structural-conflict standpoint.

The reason for this apparent contradiction is that sociological theories, especially when put into practice to explain a particular area of social life, are usually neither completely structural, nor completely interpretive. SI is a fairly moderate version of action theory which, while emphasising the primacy of interpretation in the social construction of reality, does not deny the existence of a fund of commonly-held definitions – a common culture, if you like – from which people choose their interpretations. Furthermore, the fact that it insists upon a recognition of the existence of some kind of structure of power and advantage within which the labelling of deviants takes place, also shows that it cannot be seen as adopting a fully-fledged, anti-structural position.

In this sense, SI occupies the middle ground between pure structural theory and pure action theory. In fact, as you will discover, most sociological theories are somewhere between these extremes, neither concentrating exclusively on external determinants or on interpretation, but emphasising one rather than the other. Most definitely at the interpretive extreme, however, is ethnomethodology.

## ETHNOMETHODOLOGY

Ethnomethodology pushes the action theory case – that social reality is the creation of actors – to the limit. It rests upon three assumptions:
1 Social life is inherently precarious. Anything could happen in social interaction. However:
2 Actors never realise this, because
3 They unwittingly possess the practical abilities necessary to make the world appear an ordered place.

The primary ethnomethodological interest is rather different from that of other action theorists. Instead of being concerned mainly with the *outcome* of interpretation – the creation of self-image, or the consequences of labelling, for example – it focuses on *how* interpretation is arrived at. Ethnomethodology literally means 'people's methods'. The aim is to reveal the methods used by the participants ('members') in any particular social situation to communicate to each other what they think is going on – what the situation means to them – and the efforts they each make to have this interpretation corroborated by the others. Ethnomethodology is not interested in 'the' social world, but in specific pieces of interaction between its members. The stress is on how order in a social situation is the accomplishment of its participants.

This interest in describing the practical abilities of members derives from a theory of reality called *phenomenology*. Phenomenology emphasises that things and events have no meaning in themselves. They only mean whatever human beings take them to mean. It stresses that for the members of such a meaningfully-created world to live together, meanings must be shared. Members must agree about what things are and social order depends upon shared meanings.

Members *do* share meanings. This is because of the way they interpret reality. They do so by using 'commonsense knowledge'. This is embodied in language. Through language we acquire an enormous amount of knowledge about the world, knowledge we can take for granted and which others who speak our language possess too. We have actually experienced only a tiny number of the things that we know about. The rest of the knowledge, shared with other members, is sense that is common to us all. In the words of the founder of phenomenology in sociology, Alfred Schutz (1967):

> If we put a letter in the mailbox we assume that anonymous fellow-men, called postmen, will perform a series of manipulations, unknown and unobservable to us, with the effect that the addressee, possibly also unknown to us, will receive the message and react in a way which also escapes our sensory observation; and the result of this is that we receive the book we have ordered.

Because members can take for granted this shared knowledge about reality, they can also take for granted the reality it describes. They can assume that the world is a given, objective place. It must be. After all, we *all know* what it is, and what happens in it.

This concept of shared, commonsense knowledge may sound rather like the consensus theorist's notion of culture. But culture refers to a body of rules which are *obeyed* by actors, thereby producing social order. For the ethnomethodologist commonsense knowledge is *used* by members to *create* order in a particular situation which would otherwise lack it. Ethnomethodologists define their task as showing how members do this.

Armed with commonsense knowledge and with a confident belief in the factual, ordered character of the world, members can go ahead and make sense of any situation in which they participate. Ethnomethodology stresses that each social situation is unique. The words people utter, the actions they take are *indexical* – that is, they only have sense on the particular occasion on which they are used. But they also stress that members, unwittingly engaged in identifying order and an objective reality, see things differently. They identify the similarities of an event with other events. They select from all the things happening around them evidence which supports the view that things which exist or which happen are *typical* of the world. For them, a social situation is 'a lecture', 'a dance' or 'a meeting', and a pattern is imposed on it by the application of commonsense knowledge. By commonsense knowledge too, gaps in the accounts of happenings by others are filled in by members, to reassure themselves that things are as they seem.

This is how R. J. Anderson (1979) describes Harvey Sacks' famous analysis of a two-year-old child's story:

The baby cried.
The mummy picked it up.

Sacks makes the following observations about the story:
(a) He hears the mummy as the mummy of the baby.
(b) Any other hearer will, on first hearing, hear that too. This hearing can always be revised, but it is the *first* hearing.
(c) There is a relationship between the actions described. The mummy picked up the baby because it was crying.
(d) We can all make these findings without specific knowledge of the mummy or the baby in question, nor of the child who told the story.

The import of this last observation is enormous, for if it is the case that competent users of the English language are able to find the same things from the same fragment of talk, then the methods that are used to do so must be of the highest order of generality. They must be part of the foundations of our common culture.

Without realising it, members thus create the meaning that events have. They work at making them mean something. Having arrived at an interpretation, they then have it confirmed by the corroboration of other participants. The founder of ethnomethodology, Harold Garfinkel, delighted in showing how members identify sense in occasions, even when corroboration from others is actually lacking. This is how Paul Filmer (1972) describes a very well-known Garfinkel experiment designed to demonstrate the lengths members will go to create meaning, to discover sense in an occasion, in spite of deliberate efforts to frustrate them:

Ten undergraduates were asked to participate in research being carried out by a university's department of psychiatry to explore alternative means of psychotherapy. Each was asked to discuss the background to a serious problem on which he wanted advice, and then to address to an experimenter – who had been falsely presented to him as a trainee student counsellor – a number of questions about it which would be amenable to monosyllabic 'Yes' or 'No' answers. The subject and the experimenter/counsellor were physically separated, and communicated by two-way radio. After the answer to each of his questions had been given, the subject was asked to tape-record his comments upon it, out of radio-hearing of the experimenter/counsellor. The subjects were told that it was usual to ask ten questions, and they were, of course, led to believe that they would be given bona fide answers to them. The experimenter/counsellors, however, were given a list of monosyllabic answers, evenly divided between 'yes' and 'no', but whose order had been pre-decided from a table of random numbers. Thus, in this experiment, certain crucial variables of everyday interaction situations had been neutralized: the shared language of subject and experimenter had been reduced to the verbal spoken dimension (intonation, in all probability, would also have been relatively unimportant as an agent of meaning, owing to the distortion of spoken sounds by radio); there was no chance of gestures or physical expressions intervening in the communication process because of the physical separation of subject and experimenter. Also, the possibility of the experimenter/counsellor's answers making sense to the subjects depended entirely on their interpretations of them; indeed, the possibility of answers even being those anticipated by the subjects was reduced to a matter of chance. Garfinkel publishes two unedited transcripts of the exchanges and of the subjects' comments upon them [see Garfinkel, 1967], plus a detailed explication of his interpretive findings from them. The burden of these is where the random answers to the carefully thought out and phrased questions of the subjects appeared nonsensical, irrational or in some other way inappropriate or unexpected, then the subject reinterpreted them by reformulating what he assumed to be the context of meaning he held in common with the experimenter/counsellor (and which he had attempted to communicate to the experimenter/counsellor by the phrasing and content of his questions), in order that the latter's responses made sense after all. Even where a succession of plainly contradictory answers engendered the suspicion in the subject that he was being tricked, he appeared reluctant to proceed upon the assumption that this was so.

Here, then, is a very different kind of sociology from the others we have been looking at. For structural theorists the most significant features of human social life are forces external to the individual actor. To understand social behaviour we have to understand the structural determinants of people's lives. For interactionists/ labelling theorists, the actor comes to the fore. Whether a person is in control of the interpretations of others, or is a more passive recipient of their labels, the focus is on the capacity for meaningful interaction. To understand social action we must understand the processes of interpretation that give rise to it.

For ethnomethodologists, however, the interest is different. They criticise other sociological approaches for taking for granted what they believe is actually the essence of social life. Ethnomethodology is concerned to describe the methods members use to arrive at their own understanding of social situations, though not the understanding itself. It is interested in the practice of making sense of the world, in how members accomplish social life. Though members are the architects of social order, ethnomethodology wants to know not *what* they build, but *how* they build it.

# CHAPTER SEVEN

# Language and social life: structuralism, post-structuralism, relativism and post-modernism

Language plays a pivotal role in action theory; from this point of view it is by far the most sophisticated means by which we are able to communicate our meanings to one another and thereby build what we call social order. The focus on the creative use of language by human beings reaches its extreme with ethnomethodology; here the nature of human language itself becomes the topic for sociological investigation. Thus, the technicalities of *how* it is used by humans to reveal the contents of each other's minds is the concern of the best-known ethnomethodological research device – conversational analysis. The argument is that since conversation represents the principal symbolic means by which members construct order in social situations, *how* this is done must be understood by any sociology concerned with members' methods (see pp. 97–101, 144).

For action theorists then, language and the ability to use it reflects the distinguishing feature of human life; it demonstrates our possession of consciousness and our ability to interpret, and attach meaning to, the world around us. There is a twist in the tail however. Paradoxically, an interest in language is also at the heart of a school of sociological theorising whose dedicated aim is to kill off and bury such action-theory assumptions about human beings and human social life. The aim of *structuralism* and *post-structuralism* is to bring about the *'death of the subject'* (though sometimes this enterprise is given a less gory description, when the declared aim is to *'de-centre'* the subject). It aims to point to the reasons why we should discard action theory's conception of the actor/agent/member/subject as the source of meaning and the architect of a conciously created social reality. This is also true, either implicitly or explicitly, of other forms of structural theory, like functionalism and Althusserian Marxism. However, the objections from

102

these viewpoints are rooted in their representation of societies as social structures, or systems made up of social institutions. The objections from structuralism and post-structuralism originate elsewhere. In effect, they steal the clothes from action theory and then try to strangle it with its own principal garment. These traditions agree that language *is* of vital importance for human social life, but not for the reasons action theory claims it is; the irony is that language – the very instrument which their intended victim uses to point to the triumph of the human subject's mind and conciousness in social life – is the same instrument that structuralists and post-structuralists use to try to murder and bury such claims.

## LANGUAGE IN SOCIAL LIFE

A useful starting-point from which to understand structuralism and post-structuralism is the famous stricture of philosopher Ludwig Wittgenstein against the possibility of a *private* language. As Doyal and Harris (1986) say, following Wittgenstein: 'If words did not already mean what they do mean, then they could not be used to express what you mean to say.'

Furthermore, since thought depends on languages which pre-exist us – you cannot have an idea or a concept unless you learn what to call it – thoughts themselves are social in origin. Thus, according to Wittgenstein (1973) 'you learn the concept "pain" when you learn the language.' Similarly, in answer to a question about how he knew a colour was red, Wittgenstein (1973) responded: 'It would be an answer to say I have learnt English'. As Doyal and Harris (1986) put it: 'You must learn from others the language you employ to describe even your most intimate and private feelings; thus even the way you describe yourself to yourself can only happen by using words publicly available, and learnt, by you.'

Clearly, then, we must make a distinction, as the linguist Saussure does, between *speech* – what particular individuals say to each other – and *language* – the public and social system of signs, symbols and referents which speakers have to use to think and speak. A system of language exists independently of its learners and users, and they are obliged to use the meanings referred to by its constituent symbols both to think for themselves and to exchange thoughts with others.

If all this is so, then the importance of individual thought and consciousness, so central to action sociology, is minimal; *language* determines these thoughts and it is *language* we must explain. Roger Trigg (1985) puts this argument as follows:

The nature of language and culture, viewed as systems, cannot be discovered at the level of the subject . . . this kind of structuralism offers a threat to any idea that man is the centre of the universe. The very categories of human thought are given to us . . . we can no longer be understood as subjects thinking about an independently existing world and devising language to describe it. We are not the source of language or of culture. Being human involves living in a world which has already been determined. . . .

For structuralists and post-structuralists, language thus occupies the same status as institutional structures do for Marxists and functionalists. Just as, for these theories, institutional structures exercise constraint by compelling certain kinds of belief and behaviour, so, for structuralism and post-structuralism, ways of thinking and talking which we are obliged to use exercise similar compulsion over us. In effect, our way of knowing about the world is provided for us in the languages which pre-exist us and which we learn.

The reason for using the term 'structuralism' to refer to ideas about language and its role in social life is clear; as with functionalism and Althusserian Marxism, the individual actor, agent, or subject, is irrelevant. The origin of social life lies in structural influences beyond the actor; but here it is a system of *language*, rather than a social system of functioning *institutions*, that we must understand and explain. Thus, not only does social life depend upon language, but language *defines* social reality for us.

Since language creates the world as it is experienced by actors, two obvious problems arise here. First, where does language come from? And second, does this mean that speakers of different languages inhabit different worlds?

In the work of two Frenchmen, Claude Levi-Strauss (b. 1908) an anthropologist and leading structuralist, and Michel Foucault (1926-1984), the most famous post-structuralist, we have examples of two different kinds of answers to these questions. Though Levi-Strauss is still alive and Foucault dead, Levi-Strauss's answers nonetheless came first and, as the name suggests, the *post*-structuralist (*after*-structuralism) answers of Foucault build upon this position, providing a different account.

## LEVI-STRAUSS AND STRUCTURALISM

Like his fellow Frenchman and predecessor, Emile Durkheim, Levi-Strauss argues that the structure of social life is an independent entity which constrains the behaviour and beliefs of actors. Where Levi-Strauss departs from Durkheim is in his definition of these structural constraints. For him, the defining features of human existence are (1) language, which humans encounter upon entering life, and (2) the fact that the underlying structure of all language is the same.

According to Levi-Strauss, language originates in the unconscious human mind. Since all human minds work in the same way, whatever differences languages may appear to exhibit, they are in fact organised on the same principles. Furthermore, culture is also the creation of these same unconscious thought processes; thus, the structural features of social organisation inevitably mirror those of language. In effect, according to Levi-Strauss, human thought structures the world of language and of behaviour (social organisation) in the same way.

Levi-Strauss is thus interested in the form, not the content, of language and culture. Culture, like language, is a system of signs and symbols whose organisation reflects the manner of human thought. Trigg's (1985) view of Levi-Strauss is that:

> He interprets myths and symbols in this way, saying that 'the world of symbolism is infinitely varied in content but always limited in its laws' . , , he analyses kinship systems in a similar way, viewing them as languages . . . He is concerned . . . to uncover the systems, whether of kinship or language . . . which are built by the mind, as he puts it, 'at the level of unconscious thought'.

There is nothing in social life which is the innovative creation of the conscious or imaginative mind then; human beings are not the authors of their life-stories, for these are written for them, in language and in culture. Nothing could be further from the world of Weber, Goffman, Schutz and Garfinkel.

## FOUCAULT AND POST-STRUCTURALISM

Though agreeing about the linguistic authorship of human life-stories, Foucault goes beyond the kinds of ideas produced by Levi-Strauss in two ways. First, he rejects the idea that there are *universal* features underpinning all languages. Second, he is principally interested in the

105

exercise of *power* involved in the establishment and use of a language.

Foucault follows the structuralist line in placing language at the centre of the picture. But the 'languages' in which he is interested are not the kind that are normally referred to by the term – like English, French and Spanish. He is concerned to show how specific ways of thinking and talking about aspects of the world are forms of *knowledge* which *work* like languages. He calls such 'languages' – such ways of thinking/talking – *discourses*. (This kind of approach is sometimes called *discourse theory*.) A discourse provides us with a way of *knowing* about reality; because we can only think/talk at all by using a discourse of one kind or another, a discourse provides us with our *knowledge* about the world. Furthermore, since we are compelled to know by means of discourses, they exercise *power* over us. Who we are – what we think, what we know, and what we talk about – is produced by the various discourses we encounter and use. Thus, the 'subject' – the creative, freely choosing and interpreting agent at the centre of action theory (and at the heart of philosophies like existentialism) does not exist. People's subjectivity and identity – what they think, know and talk about – is created by the discourses in which they are implicated. The post-structuralist jargon used to describe this is that the individual is *constituted* by discourses. So discourses – ways of thinking, knowing and talking – provide us with the only ways we can 'be' anybody at all. They provide us with our thoughts and our knowledge and, therefore, can be said to direct, or be behind, any actions we choose to take. This link between thought, language, knowledge and action Foucault summarises by the phrase 'discursive practices' – meaning that social life consists of activities promoted by discourses.

For Foucault, the study of history involves working out how and why different discourses came to be established when they did, because this will achieve the historian's goal – to discover why people thought, said and did what they did. According to Foucault, this is ultimately a question of power, too. The question here is: 'By what means and for what reasons did *this* form of discourse come to be established and to prevail at *this* time in history?' That is, Foucault sees the historian's task as unearthing the foundations of different discourses. The use of the archaeological metaphor is not accidental. Foucault himself describes his aim as the digging out of evidence about past discourses in an archaeological fashion; his project is literally to discover what lies underneath the emergence of various discourses.

To summarise then, Foucault's argument is that identity is constituted by discourse. People are who they are – they think what they think, know what they know, say what they say and do what they do – because of their implication in a configuration of different, and sometimes competing, discourses. The underlying reasons for the existence of these discourses can be unearthed by the historian/archaeologist; discovering these is, in essence, discovering the basis of a particular kind of knowledge and a particular kind of power. For above all, according to Foucault, the study of discourse is essentially the study of power. For Foucault then, power is exercised in two ways. Firstly, it is exercised in order that a discourse will come into being. Secondly, it is exercised *by* a discourse, since it constitutes identity – it determines what people think and know, and therefore how they act. So for Foucault, discursive practices are at the root of social life; the exercise of power through discourse is everywhere.

A brief look at Foucault's own historical work shows the sorts of factors he regards as significant in providing the foundations for the establishment of particular discourses. As a historian, Foucault has become famous for his accounts of the history of medicine, madness, sexuality, punishment and the body, in terms of the various discourses that have defined these phenomena. He argues that the emergence of particular ways of knowing and talking about such areas of social life depend on the prior existence of specific organisational and institutional arrangements. For example, he argues that it was only the appearance of the clinic that made medical discourse possible. Because we now live in a world where the presence of medical concepts and their use in various areas of social life is taken for granted, it is a little difficult for us to appreciate just how pervasive such a discourse has become. For us, notions of 'health' and 'ill-health' are not just applied to bodies, but to societies (Durkheim), desires, sexual orientations, appetites, pastimes, interests, families, marriages, economies, and so forth. This list shows how contagious (another use of medical discourse!) the use of such concepts has become. It therefore draws attention to the constitution of thinking and consciousness that Foucault argues discourse can achieve. It is evidence of the power of both the discourse, and the practitioners who benefit from such a way of knowing about the world.

The emergence of the idea of madness as illness is another good example. The interpretation of 'mad' as 'without reason' is a feature of a discourse facilitated by the emergence of Enlightenment views about the virtue of reason and rationality, and the possibility of progress via science – that is, by the creation of ideas of modernity. Yet madness was not deemed to be 'illness' until rather later when, in effect, it then became *another* condition to be consumed by medical discourse. In Medieval Europe the eradication of leprosy left the buildings used to confine lepers empty. This provided the circumstances for the possibility of the exclusion from ordinary society of other categories of persons – particularly the 'insane'. The creation of asylums made possible the discipline of psychiatry, with the result that mental 'illness', the mental hospital, psychiatry and psychiatrists all grew up alongside one another. Although the exercise of the power to incarcerate people now defined as 'sick' is deemed to be 'therapy' and the provision of 'medical treatment', the net effect, i.e. the social control of people exhibiting behaviour disturbing to others, is the same as it ever was, except that now *medical* discourse provides the justification for control, via *hospitalisation*.

This is quintessential Foucault. As we have seen throughout the book so far, the task for theorists engaged in the project of modernity is to generate knowledge which can then be used to enable societal progress and make possible individual freedom and liberation. For Foucault, however, forms of knowledge are used to oppress, control and coerce. Thus he turns the modernist definition of knowledge on its head, saying that we can only know reality through discourse, but that this knowledge also controls who we are. We do not use knowledge to create better worlds; social change simply means the emergence of new discourses, which in turn define and control subjects in new ways. These 'new' ways of knowing are not 'better' or 'worse' than what has gone before – they are simply different, reflecting different forms of power. Defining madness as the possession of sacred knowledge, as representing lack of reason, or as evidence of a diseased mind, is not a matter of 'falsehoods' being replaced by 'truth'. It is simply a shift in power relations – the replacement of one way of defining reality by another. Foucault's thinking is thus a good example of *relativism*.

## RELATIVISM

A relativist believes there is no such thing as 'objective' truth; there are only competing ways of looking at things and competing ways of knowing about things. As Pascal put it: 'What is truth on one side of the Pyrenees can be falsehood on the other.' 'Reality' thus has no meaning apart from what is *believed* to be real by some groups of believers. Though it is perhaps hard for us to grasp because of the way we embrace modernism, take science and scientific knowledge for granted, and regard them as 'superior' to other forms of knowledge, the relativist would argue that even scientific knowledge and practice – scientific discourse, as Foucault would call them – cannot be said to be objectively superior to other forms of knowledge which are believed to be true in other times and places. Thus, says the relativist, believing in the notion that the world is as it is because God made it that way, that witchcraft causes misfortune, that the conjunction of the planets can cure warts, or whatever, is not a belief in falsehoods *except from the point of view of another definition* (in this case scientific) *of truth*. Even though we live in a world where scientific discourse prevails this does not mean that it is *therefore superior* to other claims for truth. For relativists, it is the other way round; scientific knowledge is not powerful because it is true; *it is true because it is powerful*. Thus the question is not '*What* is true?' but 'How did *this* version of what is true come to dominate in *these* social and historical circumstances?' It is a question, in fact, for the sociology, politics and history of knowledge. (See pages 155–9 for a further discussion of these issues).

This sort of argument is the very antithesis of the claims about knowledge made by proponents of the 'project of modernity'. As we have seen, for modernists the application of reason, exemplified by science, enables humans to discover *the* truth about the nature of reality, to understand the causes of social life in the way natural science has revealed the workings of nature. Such knowledge allows us the chance of progress, social development and individual liberation and freedom. The more we discover, the better we can construct our world; the more we know, the greater our opportunities for human emancipation.

We have already explained the views of Max Weber, for whom the construction of modern, rational society represented the imprisonment and destruction of the human spirit. Relativists too, though for different reasons, also cast profound doubt on the optimistic assumptions underpinning the idea of modernity. Since from this viewpoint 'truth' is relative and a product of the historical and social world in which we are implicated, knowledge itself has to be understood as socially constructed. For relativists, there is no way of acquiring any *certainty* about reality. Truth and knowledge are culturally and historically specific; whatever we 'know' is constructed for us – it is the product of the time in history and the location of the world in which we find ourselves. Whatever structural sociology we use – whether we define the process whereby we acquire truths as a product of interconnecting discourses, as socialisation into prevailing ideas, as ideological indoctrination, or whatever – the relativist cannot escape the fact that what we are and what we know is a social creation. Indeed, from this point of view, locked as we inevitably are in the discourses/traditions of time and place, the fact that we are constituted by such phenomena means we have no way of standing back and making objective judgements anyway. For even the criteria by which we judge truth or falsehood are *themselves* social constructions, provided for us by our social world. As Feyerabend (1981) puts it: 'Each tradition, each form of life, has its own standards of judging human behaviour . . . a citizen will use the standards to which he belongs: Hopi standards, if he is a Hopi:

109

fundamentalist Protestant standards, if he is a fundamentalist.'

For a relativist then, even 'objectivity' – the scientist's plumbline – is relative. Bloor (1981) describes it as follows:

> Suppose the tribe on this side of the river worship one god, and the tribe on the other side of the river worship another god. If the worship of the god is a stable feature of tribal practice, if they are spoken of routinely, if courses of action are justified by reference to them, then I would say both beliefs are objective.

## POST-MODERNISM

If this sort of relativist argument is correct, then for the project of modernity it is catastrophic. The argument is that although our 'socialness' makes ordered life possible, it nonetheless denies us the chance of ever knowing 'reality' except from our point of view. The construction of sociological theories does not beckon the dawning of truth and liberty then, for these prescriptions are themselves social products and cannot be said to be right or wrong – just different.

The implications of this sort of relativist argument have led some commentators to argue that we should abandon any hope of acquiring truth or knowledge about an objective reality, and accept that all sociological accounts – even *all* humanly-constructed accounts of reality – have equal validity. No one, over-arching theory can point the way to a modern Utopia; we have gone beyond the time when we should believe that such a *meta-narrative*, or grand account of *all* history and *all* social life, like functionalism or Marxism, can have any credibility. We must therefore accept we are in a *post-modern* world, where grand theoretical designs are obsolete, and where it is inevitable that multiple claims to truth compete with each other for our support. The fact that some of these theories, like Foucault's, claim that we have no choice about what we do think, whereas others disagree, does not change the truth about the pluralistic character of knowledge. For post-modernists, in fact, this is the *only* truth. Their argument is that we must accept that modernist concepts like reason and progress provide us with no purchase at all on the way we live, or the way we will live in the future.

Post-modern thinking applies not only to social organisations, but to all other realms of human activity and production, like art, architecture, and literature for example. Here again, the focus is on pluralism and on competing accounts of the nature of virtue, style, truth and falsehood. It is also on the impermanence and instability of such definitions – the

110

transcience of certainties and the chronically brief life of truths. Post-modernism thus represents a reaction to the Enlightenment-sponsored modern search for *the* truth, ultimate meaning, and *the* nature of reality. Instead, the superficial and ephemeral nature of contemporary human life is emphasised, where, because of the persistently impermanent character of claims to truth, it is fashion, trend and image which have come to matter more than substance and meaning. In particular, the cultural dominance of the mass media is emphasised, where reality and identity are constructed for us by advertising, popular music and television soap operas. So although the mass media shrinks our world, because of its ability to transcend time and space, this gives us no more meaningful a purchase on 'reality' – it simply multiplies the number, frequency and impermanence of the accounts of reality we consume. What we 'see' via the media inevitably constitutes a major source of our knowledge in a post-modern world – but what we see and know, and therefore are, is merely for here and now, and only until another story comes along.

# CHAPTER EIGHT

# *Theory, knowledge and explanation*

So far we have portrayed sociology as a subject of diverse theories. There is no theoretical orthodoxy; there are only competing ways of explaining the nature of the relationship between the individual and society. We now turn to an equally important issue: how do different sociologists arrive at the evidence they use to support their respective claims for truth? That is, what are the procedures used by sociologists to generate the knowledge on which their explanations are based?

To begin to address these issues, we need to define some important terms. First, *methodology* and *method* refer to different levels of knowledge acquisition; methodology refers to the knowledge *production* process while method refers to specific *tools* of knowledge acquisition. The difference is the same as that apparent between two aspects of gardening. A gardener has to have:

(a) an overall strategy for getting the most out of a garden – as in deciding when and where to dig, plant, fertilise, water, prune and cut back – and also;

(b) specific tools to achieve this overall aim, such as a spade, fork, trowel, watering-can, fertiliser, hoe, and so on.

The analogy is plain; a methodology is a knowledge producer's overall strategy, while his or her methods are the specific tools used to achieve this task.

## METHODS

In a sociologist's tool shed, there are many instruments of data collection, which include:

(a) *Question-asking*, by means of an *interview* as part of a *survey*; this can be *structured, focused* (semi-structured) or *unstructured*. The degree of structure refers to the extent to which each interviewee, or *respondent*, is asked exactly the same questions put to him/her in

112

exactly the same way. The more structured the question-asking, the easier it is to measure and compare answers, and thereby produce *quantitative* data. The more unstructured the question-asking is, the greater the depth of understanding is possible about the respondent, and descriptive, *qualitative* data is more likely to be produced.

(b) *Questionnaires*, lists of questions on paper, are answered in writing by each respondent. Clearly, questionnaires are completely structured and the results are easily quantifiable.

(c) *Sampling techniques* allow you to select a small number of respondents to question. These answers, because of the way the sample has been selected, can be said to accurately represent the whole population from which the sample has been drawn.

(d) *Focus groups*, consisting of between six and eight people and guided by a moderator, generate discussion-based data, and can be useful in gaining insight into the way certain categories of similarly placed actors feel and think about issues relevant to them.

(e) *Observation* also enables the production of *ethnographic*, or *qualitative* data. Such descriptive accounts can be generated by *participant* or *non-participant observation*, and the subjects can either be aware of the fact they are being observed (*overt observation*) or not (*covert observation*). Observation may also be visually or electronically recorded.

(f) The *experiment* makes use of a social setting which has been artificially created in order to identify the impact on social behaviour of specific influences which are of interest to the experimenter; the idea is to *isolate* these influences and measure their effect in a way not possible in the real world.

All the above are examples of *primary* data collection techniques; their product is actively generated by the researcher. *Secondary* data collection involves the use of data assembled for other purposes:

(a) *Official statistics* are compiled by governmental or other organisations and are *sociographic* accounts of aspects of human life, as in the case of the Census, or statistics about health, divorce, crime, educational achievement, and so on.

(b) *Content analysis* involves the examination and measurement of *textual*, *oral* or *visual* accounts of human social life, generated for non-sociological purposes in books, newspapers and magazines, for audio broadcast, or for television or film.

(c) *Documentary source analysis* not only takes an interest in documents like official papers, but also in personal effects, such as letters, essays and diaries.

(d) *Cultural analysis* takes an interest in any form of human product –

clothes, images, music, language and such like – that functions as a means of symbolic representation. The job of the cultural researcher is the qualitative one of *decoding* the meanings of these cultural symbols – translating the language used to communicate.

(e) *Deconstruction* refers to the controversial *post-structuralist* method of showing how the language used in texts cannot be assumed to mean just what its author wants it to mean; the project of the deconstructionist is to show how texts always convey more meaning than any one person, author or critic, can understand or control.

## ONTOLOGY AND EPISTEMOLOGY

Knowing how these instruments work and the kinds of knowledge they can produce is only part of the problem, however. Of equal importance is *why* they are used – what the purposes of the sociological researcher are. The same research methods can be used for very different ends; what matters is not so much what a method is *technically* capable of doing, but what particular task it is asked to do. After all, knowing what a knife *can* do – from balancing peas to cutting up food to opening envelopes to slitting throats to making surgical incisions – doesn't tell us *what* it does on any particular occasion, unless we know the aim and intention of the user.

Similarly, there is little *inherent* quality in a research tool; what matters is the uses to which the sociological researcher chooses to put it. To understand the use of data collection techniques, we have to understand the context in which they are employed; this context is often revealed by understanding the *ontological* and the *epistemological* interests of the researcher.

In any kind of knowledge production by human beings, much depends on your *ontology* – your definition of your *subject-matter*, or what you take *reality* to be like. Your *epistemology* – what you count as *knowledge* – depends upon what you want knowledge *about*. Furthermore, it is often the case that the nature of the knowledge you want determines the *methodology* and *methods* you use to acquire it. Let us look at a non-sociological example of these relationships.

## KNOWING ABOUT ILLNESS: SOME COMPARISONS

In our culture, when people feel ill we usually presume that there is something the matter with the body; that is, for us, sickness is normally deemed to have *organic* origins. Furthermore, to gain knowledge of such organic disease, we use medical investigative procedures to discover *empirical* evidence of its existence – that is, evidence identifiable by the human senses. Such evidence is generated by the physical examination of bodily phenomena like blood, excreta, or fragments of tissue from the organs believed to be affected by the illness. Such procedures are intended to reveal the nature of the organic lesion producing the feeling of ill-health, and cure is effected by medical counter-measures, such as drugs or surgical intervention.

So, if my throat is sore, I assume there is something wrong with my respiratory system. To get physical evidence of this, a throat swab is taken and its contents examined in a pathology laboratory; the idea is to reveal the presence of the bacteria causing the infection, and to allow an appropriate antibiotic to be administered. The relationship is thus:

| | |
|---|---|
| ontological assumptions | illness is organic |
| ↓ | ↓ |
| epistemological assumptions | empirical evidence (from physical examination of the body) |
| ↓ | ↓ |
| methodology/method | experimentation and observation in the controlled conditions of a laboratory. |

Even in our culture, however, there are alternative ways of knowing about, and therefore explaining, the same phenomenon, which can lead to different procedures being undertaken. If I were to consult a psychotherapist about my illness rather than a GP, a different course of action may well be undertaken because of the different set of ontological assumptions about the nature of reality held by such therapists.

*Psychotherapy*, as its name suggests, is a form of treatment based on a theory of human behaviour, and of illness in particular, which is interested in the mind and its effects on the body. From this point of view, the possibility that a physical condition like a sore throat may have mental origins must be explored. If this is the case, physical intervention to eradicate bacteria in the throat is not a cure of the *cause* of the condition, only a temporary alleviation of the *symptoms*. For a psychotherapist, since the organic lesion is the symptom of a mental condition – say stress, tension or depression – intervention to eradicate these phenomena is necessary. Many psychotherapists insist that while physical symptoms can be treated by physical, drug-based intervention, the causes of these symptoms have to be treated at the level of the non-physical, at the level of human consciousness, by counselling therapies such as psychoanalysis, by cognitive therapy (intervention in the pattern and content of the patient's thinking), or behaviour therapy (modifying the patient's behaviour). Here the relationship is:

| | |
|---|---|
| ontological assumptions | illness is emotionally caused |
| ↓ | ↓ |
| epistemological assumptions | oral evidence is needed about aspects of the patient's life, experiences, and relationships |
| ↓ | ↓ |
| methodology/method | counselling, psychoanalysis, and so on |

Among the Azande, an African tribe famous in anthropological literature, an even bigger difference in ontological assumptions about reality leads to the acquisition of different forms of knowledge in order to establish explanations of the world. For the Azande, most forms of misfortune, including illness, are caused by witchcraft, which they call *mangu*. This is believed to be a physical substance which lives in the intestines of human beings. The human (witch) inhabited by witchcraft need not be aware of its presence, but since mangu is the cause of the misfortunes of others, their well-being depends upon knowing who the witch among them is. This is especially so in the case of illness; the sick person cannot expect to get better until the witch is identified and appropriate measures have been taken. Since witchcraft works most effectively over short distances, the most likely host of the mangu causing your illness is someone socially and/or physically close to the afflicted person. In the event of a misfortune like an illness then, it is not a matter of seeking organic or emotional causes, but of identifying mangu inside someone else's body.

This is done by consulting an *oracle*. The most influential oracle is a poison oracle, or *benge*. It provides the knowledge required by answering 'yes' or 'no' to questions put to it. The idea is that a person is selected who might be host to the mangu and the oracle is asked if this is right. Upon asking the question, poison is fed to a chick; the fate of the chick provides an answer. Should you ask the chick to die if your suspect is the witch but it lives, your selection is wrong and you must try again; if it dies, you are right. The testing process is carried out until evidence has been obtained. (Clearly, one of the things not to be in Azandeland is a young chicken.)

Having obtained the truth, the unsuspecting witch is informed. However dismayed or incredulous the witch may feel, he or she is obliged to expel the mangu by ritually blowing water out of his or her mouth. In the case of a misfortune like the crops failing, there is now an explanation. In the case of illness, the sick person can now be expected to get better. Of course, people spontaneously recover from most illnesses, which serves to reinforce faith in the explanatory system. If illness persists, however, it is either assumed that the original witch was not sincere in his or her attempts to rid him or herself of the mangu, or that another witch has taken over the prosecution of the misfortune. In either case, the oracle is used again to collect further proof. In the event of illness leading to death – all deaths are by definition caused by witchcraft – it is still necessary to find the (final) witch. This is done by instructing an expert witch-doctor to practise his magic against the unknown witch; the next person to die can then be said to be that witch.

Though alien to us, such an explanatory system contains exactly the same elements, in the same relationships, as systems with which we are more familiar:

| | |
|---|---|
| ontological assumptions | misfortune is caused by witchcraft |
| ↓ | ↓ |
| epistemological assumptions | empirical evidence is needed of who the witch is |
| ↓ | ↓ |
| methodology/method | consultation with an oracle or witchdoctor |

The point is that however great the differences in content between these different explanatory systems might be, the form which they take is the same. We must now see whether this is also true of the various explanatory systems which use sociological knowledge.

## SOCIOLOGICAL THEORIES – ONTOLOGICAL AND EPISTEMOLOGICAL IMPLICATIONS

The sociological theories we look at in this book can certainly be identified with specific ontological and epistemological assumptions. We summarise these connections in the table shown overleaf:

| Theory | Ontology | Epistemology |
|---|---|---|
| Durkheim and functionalists | Reality is a normative or cultural system (a system of ideas) which produces social life whose workings are independent of human consciousness | Appropriate knowledge is *empirical* evidence of the structural forces which produce behaviour and beliefs |
| Marx and Marxists | Reality is an economically dominated social system whose workings are (a) independent of human consciousness ( Althusserian Marxism), or (b) independent of human consciousness except ultimately when structural change comes about through political action | Since modes of production are real forces *underlying* social life and are not, therefore, empirically evident, appropriate knowledge is a *theoretical* understanding of the workings of these systems |
| Weber and Weberians | Reality is a historically unique, but meaningfully created, set of structural circumstances | Appropriate knowledge is *Verstehen*-generated evidence of the social activities which have produced historically unique structural formations |
| Feminists | Reality is constituted by the various sets of structural constraints which subordinate and oppress women | Appropriate knowledge is that which allows women to speak for themselves, rather than knowledge about men's worlds, which presumes itself to be about women's worlds too |
| Interpretivists/ action theorists | Reality is the meaningful accomplishment of social actors | Appropriate knowledge is an understanding of the motivations and methods underlying meaningfully created social settings |
| Giddens and structuration theory | Reality has a dual character: structures both constrain, and enable, human agents to exercise choice and thereby reproduce, or redefine, these structures | Appropriate knowledge is that which allows us to explain social structures *and* provides an understanding of the human agency which takes place in the context of these structures |
| Post-structuralists | Reality is a configuration of discursive practices which constitute – exercise power over – subjects | Appropriate knowledge provides contemporary and historical evidence of the way discourses constitute subject identity and social reality |

So far so good. But the big research question is whether these ontological and epistemological connections among different sociological theories *also* lead to the use of specific methodologies – particular research strategies – and to specific uses of data collection techniques. Here, things are not so clear-cut.

One of the reasons for this is that some of the most notable contributions to sociological knowledge have been intellectual and rational in character, concerned exclusively with ontology and epistemology, rather than involving the systematic collection of evidence. C. Wright Mills called these 'grand theories' and some of the works of Durkheim, Marx and Weber, and of some twentieth-century writers like Parsons, Giddens and Althusser, clearly fall into this category.

But even in versions of sociology which *do* rely on data collection for evidence, the connection between specific theories and specific methods is not always straightforward. We can summarise the connections as follows:

(1) Theoretical commitment *can* be the reason for the choice of research procedures, but;

(2) sometimes methodologies and methods are chosen for *non-theoretical* reasons, particularly practical and political ones, and;

(3) in recent years, collaboration between old theoretical opponents has given a new impetus to the use of particular methods.

To understand why, we need to tell the story of developments in sociological research in the nineteenth and twentieth centuries.


## A BRIEF HISTORY OF SOCIOLOGICAL RESEARCH

During the telling of this story, the following elements to the plot will become apparent:

(1) In both the nineteenth and the twentieth centuries, a major factor has been the influence of *science* on the production of sociological knowledge.

(2) A particular form of science, based on a philosophy called *positivism*, dominated sociological research for the first half of the twentieth century. This was mainly because the ontological and epistemological preoccupations of positivism perfectly matched those of sociology's dominant theory during that time – consensus theory/functionalism. Because of the intimacy of their relationship, once functionalism came under attack in the 1960s (see pp. 39–42), so did positivism.

119

(3) Two main principles of positivist philosophy are that;

(a) Only *empirical* evidence, identifiable by human experience (obtained by using the senses) can be relied upon to provide demonstrable proof of reality.

(b) Such knowledge of reality must be generated in an *objective* way, dealing only with facts and free from contamination by any value judgements or *subjective* factors.

In effect, positivism insists that any claim to knowledge must rest solely on what *is*, on what can be *shown* to be the case; opinions, preferences or choices are completely excluded.

(4) From the 1960s onwards, these two aspects of positivist philosophy began to be criticised, both from within sociology and from outside.

(a) *The anti-positivism of action sociology*
Action theory opposed the reliance on empirical evidence in positivist sociology, claiming that since an interest in actors' ideas and interpretations – non-empirical, mental phenomena – is at the heart of the sociological enterprise, sociology cannot be a positivist science (see pp. 137–52).

(b) *The anti-positivism of realism*
*Realism* is a philosophy of science which argues that positivism provides a false account of scientific activity, since *no* form of science relies exclusively on empirical evidence. Realists say there are always aspects of any form of reality which remain hidden from empirical view, beneath the surface of what *is* capable of being experienced. So, from this point of view, the fact that action sociology wants to focus on non-empirical phenomena, like ideas and beliefs, does not render this activity incapable of being scientific, since, for the realist, *all* sciences have to deal with such phenomena (see pp. 153–4).

(c) *The anti-positivism of Thomas Kuhn*
The work of the historian of science, Thomas Kuhn, represents an assault on the positivist claim that an objective, value-free form of *any* kind of scientific knowledge production is possible. Kuhn's argument is that once you look at any scientific activity close up, it is much more like other forms of human production – influenced by preference, judgement and subjectivity, partisanship and politics – than positivists claim. The relevance to sociology of Kuhn's critique is that it defines even scientific knowledge as a *social* construction –

120

the product of a time and place, and of socially generated choices, based on particular values (see pp. 155–9).

(5) The action critique of positivist sociology reflected a theoretical and methodological rift between structural and interpretive sociologists which dominated the subject throughout the 1960s. At that time, it could truly be said that methods *were* chosen because of a commitment to one side or the other in the conflict. From the 1970s onwards, however, three distinct attempts to bring about an end to, if not a resolution of, this conflict can be identified, and the theory/method relationship in social research became more complicated.

(a) *Triangulation* has characterised much social research. This term refers to the deliberate use of a variety of theoretical positions and of research procedures in particular projects, a move at least in part designed to satisfy the ontological, epistemological and methodological sensibilities of both structural and action theorists.

(b) The need to secure *funding* for research has encouraged the two sides to seek some sort of peace, if not a reconciliation. While the 1960s' expansion in British sociology brought with it considerable financial support for research in the subject, during the 1970s, and especially during the Thatcherite 1980s, the well virtually dried up. In such straitened circumstances, methods began to be chosen for their cost-effectiveness rather than for their congruence with particular theoretical interests. In addition, projects began to be designed to be *politically* attractive – to appeal to the prejudices of the funding agencies (often as the result of government pressure) – rather than being dedicated to the support of one particular theoretical or methodological position and against others (see pp. 162–4).

(c) At a theoretical level, Anthony Giddens introduced the concept of *structuration*, intended to convey the idea that both structure *and* action constitute social life. Giddens argues that structures not only constrain actors, but also *enable* them to make choices and act meaningfully. Furthermore, while motivated action can merely reproduce the structural contexts in which actors live their lives, they can also be transformed by such action (see pp. 164–6).

(6) Three other developments in the practice of social research from the 1980s onwards must also be mentioned:

(a) *Cultural analysis* has employed semiotics – the study of signs – to decode the social use of cultural items as symbolic forms of representation (see pp. 166–8).

(b) In a similar vein, *post-structuralists* have argued that since the principal form of symbolic representation – language – drives human life, ancient divisions between disciplines like philosophy, sociology, literary analysis, psychoanalysis and history are irrelevant, since all are ultimately concerned with revealing the uses of language in both text and image (see pp. 168–70).

(c) Some *feminists* have developed research strategies and techniques specifically tailored to give women a proper sociological voice; here research methods have been chosen because of their ability to fulfil this *political* purpose (see pp. 172–4).

Let us now look at these various strands, beginning with the role of science in nineteenth-century sociology.

# CHAPTER NINE

# *Sociology and science*

## MODERNITY AND SCIENCE

Because the idea of modernity is substantially concerned with the benefits of rational thought, and of scientific thinking and practice in particular, it is unsurprising that the classic commentators on modern society took a great interest in science. As we have seen, Durkheim (1938) followed Comte in being dedicated to establishing sociology as a 'positive science of society', using the positivist procedures which had paid dividends for natural science as a means of establishing laws of social life. This scientific knowledge, argued Durkheim, could be the political tool by which peaceful, harmonious, stable societies could be engineered.

Marx, too, was committed to using science to achieve political progress. Two differences from Durkheim's positivism are apparent in his work, though. First, he was no empiricist in the positivistic sense of seeking observable evidence of structural forces through the measurement of the incidence of regularities of thought and action. Marx's interest was in the economic forces lying beneath the surfaces of observable events, not capable of empirical identification, but only of being understood at the level of theory. This form of science – known as *realism* – rests upon the view that the reality with which science is concerned exists as a set of 'generative mechanisms', producing observable behaviour and action, but not themselves directly observable (see pp. 153–4).

Second, Marx, like Weber, uses historical comparisons as the major source of evidence. To prove his point about historical materialism, Marx is unable to conduct experiments or carry out surveys; what he has to do is marshal the historical evidence of a number of different societal forms and, by systematically comparing these, to persuade us of the truth of his historical analysis.

Weber also uses historical comparative analysis and he too, is determined to show how science can be used for humanity's benefit. But his science is interested in revealing the role of social *action* in constructing social life and in producing historical events; Weber thus argues that proper sociological reasoning should both be 'causally and meaningfully adequate', showing how people's interpretation of the world, which produces meaningful action, is also the cause of empirically observable social formations. For Weber, science is about the examination of the real world by using *Verstehen* in order to assess the validity of the ideal-typical constructions of the sociologist. Unlike the positivist, Weber saw objective accounts of the world as essentially based on subjective (ideal-typical) selections from an infinite reality. Objectivity is not possible at the stage of selection, then, only at the validation, or testing, stage of the *Verstehen*-produced hypotheses of the observer.

Weber differs from Durkheim and Marx on the question of science in another way, too. According to him, the rationalisation of the modern world is essentially about the dominance of calculability, and the exemplar of calculative thinking is scientific thinking. Once again, there is an apparent paradox in Weber's work; science – the very means of establishing objective accounts of reality – is also, in the end, the perfect example of the *dehuman* and the *anti-spiritual*, which caused Weber so much pessimism for the future of life under modernity.


## POSITIVISM AND SOCIOLOGY

In the first half of the twentieth century, mainly through the work of Americans such as Parsons, Durkheim's theoretical and epistemological interests won the day and so too, did his view of the importance of positivistic procedures in generating knowledge of social forces. Let us look in detail at the nature of this positivist enterprise.

*Ontology*

For a positivist, any form of reality is made up of phenomena in causal relations with one another – the world consists of things causing other things. The existence of one particular phenomenon is explained by identifying another phenomenon as its cause; furthermore, the effect of this cause may well in turn cause *other* phenomena to be as they are. Things are therefore in an endless, and invariable, chain of causal relationships.

This world is an *objective* entity, and our feelings about it do not change the way it is. Whether we like it or not, water *will* freeze at a certain temperature. Whether we like it or not, the temperature *is* higher in the summer than in the winter. Whether we like it or not, leaves *will* fall from deciduous trees in the autumn. Human attitudes or values about reality, while they are bound to exist, should therefore have no part to play in revealing the cause and effect relationships which make it up; what we would *like* to be the case, or what we think *ought* to be the case have no relevance for the way the world *is*. Science must therefore proceed in a wholly *objective* fashion and exclude any subjective factors based on human value-judgements.

## Epistemology

Knowledge of this objective world must be *empirical* – capable of being apprehended by the senses – if we are to persuade others of the truth of our accounts. Only *demonstrable* proof of our explanations of reality is acceptable; asking others to have faith in our answers, or to trust us in our claims that we are right, has no place in science if we cannot provide empirical evidence in support of our claims.

## Methodology

The research process favoured by positivism is known as the *hypothetico-deductive* method. The stages in this methodology are as follows. From existing knowledge – what is – the scientist speculates about what might also be. This is called the deduction of an *hypothesis* (which explains the methodology's title). For example, say we know that, on average, men contract lung cancer more often than women. Suppose we also know that, on average, men smoke more cigarettes than women. Knowing these facts, we might well speculate – *hypothesise* – that smoking causes lung cancer. It is not that there are no other potential (hypothetical) explanations of these facts. For example, it could be that men tend to work at jobs which make lung cancer more likely. Or men may have some sort of biological predisposition towards cancer which women do not possess. There are always plenty of alternative, competing, hypotheses of the causes of things; scientists have to choose the explanation they think most likely.

Having arrived at an hypothesis, the scientist then tries to assess its *validity*, or truth, by testing it against the empirical evidence. Two versions of this enterprise exist – *confirmationism* and *falsificationism*. Confirmationist testing involves collecting as much support in favour of the hypothesis as possible; the more times the hypothesis is supported by the evidence, the more confidence we can have in it. Falsificationist testing works the other way round; instead of trying to *prove* the hypothesis, the scientist tries to *disprove* it. This is based on the argument, put most forcibly by philosopher Karl Popper, that it does not matter how many times you prove something to be true, as you can never be sure you will not disprove it next time. So, since final confirmation of the truth is unavailable, the project should be turned on its head; science should be about *disproof* – the aim of research should be to *falsify* an hypothesis. Popper's famous example of the non-availability of truth concerns swans; no matter how many thousands of white swans you may have observed, you cannot be *certain* all swans are white, for the next one you see may be black. And if you do observe a black one, this is the only certainty you can claim – that all swans are *not* white. Einstein summarised this by saying that while thousands of scientists could not prove him *right*, it only needed one to prove him *wrong*. Science should therefore be about the search for new and more sophisticated ways of *disproving*; the longer a scientific story remains unfalsified, the more confidence we can have in it – though we can never be finally *certain*.

## Method

Scientific investigation involves the testing of the validity of an hypothesis by means of the *experiment*. Though some sciences, like astronomy and meteorology, test hypotheses by observing phenomena in their natural environment alone, most sciences involve experimentation.

A scientific experiment involves removing the phenomena in which you are interested (the experimental *variables*) from their natural setting and examining them, under controlled conditions, in a laboratory. The idea is that since an hypothesis specifies a cause and effect relationship between particular variables – the *independent* variable is said to cause the effect on the *dependent* variable – these variables should be examined in isolation from others. When variables irrelevant to the hypothesis (*extraneous* variables) are not present, but an hypothesised effect comes about, the hypothesis has been supported. The aim of an experiment is to *measure*, or *quantify*, the extent to which a cause and effect relationship exists. According to Cuff, Payne *et al.* (1979):

> In the ideal experiment, the scientist can control all important variables except one, and then see what happens when that one is varied. For example, if we wish to study the effects of a certain chemical on the growth of runner beans, or if we wish to test a specific hypothesis to the effect that the presence of this chemical and plant growth have a stated relationship, then 'all' other factors, for example, sunlight, water, seed, soil, must be the same for all the sample plots. Then, the varying amounts of the chemical on different test plots can be held responsible for the different growth rates

observed of the runner beans. By controlling the conditions, that is 'other factors', we have a method of observing and comparing which allows us to infer (and quantify the extent of) specific causal relationships.

In effect then, positivism is an *expert-centred* approach to explaining reality. The subject of investigation is a story about the world made up by the scientist; hypotheses are creations of the observer, and are tested by the observer. The world as it is perceived by its inhabitants is irrelevant; the inanimate and animate phenomena which make up the natural world do not have the characteristics they do because of any choice on their part – they are involuntarily obeying laws of nature. Science is about revealing the empirical evidence of these laws by utilising 'expert' insights based on pre-existing theoretical knowledge; scientific knowledge is *about* the theories of the expert observers, collected *by* these experts.

What is contentious about positivist *sociology* is the claim that these scientific assumptions and procedures, which may work very well in the natural sciences, should be applied to *social* life. Here the questions are:

(a) Is social life best understood ontologically as a world of phenomena in cause and effect relationships?
(b) Can we best explain human behaviour by relying exclusively on empirical evidence?
(c) Is it possible for a social scientist to match the rigour of the laboratory experiment in investigating social worlds?
(d) Most important of all, should we ignore the theories of their world held by social actors in favour of expert, observer-centred accounts? Such a view of science might apply where the phenomena in which we are interested possess no consciousness, and therefore no theories of their own, but can these ontological, epistemological and methodological aims be sustained when the subject-matter is thinking, interpreting humanity?

Positivist sociologists say 'yes' to all these questions. Action theorists say 'no'.


## POSITIVIST SOCIOLOGY

*Ontology*

Though aspects of positivist philosophy have been employed by a variety of structural approaches, the most enthusiastic positivists in sociology have been theorists who see an ontological identity between nature and society – consensus theorists. As we have seen, it is the consensus theorist's view that, although human beings have their own theories about their worlds, exercised through their consciousness, these *non-empirical* entities can be ignored in favour of observer theories of the structural forces which produce behaviour and belief. Just as the phenomena which make up the natural world do not *choose* to be as they are, neither, for consensus theorists, do the choices, interpretations and ideas of human beings have any relevance to the character of their social lives. For consensus theory, we do not *choose* to believe the things we believe, or to act in the way we act. We *learn* to think and to do these things; pre-existing cultural rules *determine* our ideas and behaviour through socialisation. Thus, in the same way that natural phenomena are the product of laws of nature, so people's ideas and actions are caused by those external social forces which make up social structures. Because of the ontological similarity between nature and society, consensus theorists argue that the means by which they are investigated should be similar too.

*Epistemology*

Here the need is for demonstrable proof – empiricism is the key to social scientific certainty, as it is for all sciences. For the positivist sociologist, the route to empirical evidence of the *social facts* of people's lives, as Durkheim called them, is the *quantification* of the extent of *regularities* of behaviour and belief. Since behaviour and belief are determined by external structural forces, we should collect evidence by counting the number of times people do things, or think things. What we then have is statistical (empirical) evidence to help us to explain the forces that have produced this behaviour and belief.

*Methodology*

Once social life is measured and quantified statistically, a social science can proceed just like a natural science, by using the hypothetico-deductive method; hypotheses can be tested against empirical evidence. The big problem concerns the testing process, however. Positivist sociology has favoured the use of three research tools in particular to do this: the experiment, observation and, most often, the survey.

# METHODS OF DATA COLLECTION IN POSITIVIST SOCIOLOGY

THE EXPERIMENT

There are obvious problems with testing sociological hypotheses by experimentation.

(a) If people know they are being experimented on, they may change their behaviour – the *'observer effect'*.
(b) If they are denied knowledge of the experiment to minimise this effect – if, for instance, the research is covert – ethical issues come to the fore.
(c) Experiments can only concern themselves with extremely small-scale interaction.

Most sociological research cannot avoid these problems. Sociologists are interested in family behaviour, achievement in education, behaviour in the workplace, and so on. Even if they would let us, there would be no point in extracting members of families, schoolchildren, car workers and others from their normal social settings to observe them under experimental conditions and get empirical evidence of their behaviour. Obviously, they will only exhibit the behaviour in which we are interested in their normal surroundings – at home, school, or work. To gain evidence of the impact of structural forces in everyday social settings, positivist sociologists have sometimes used *observation* as a data-collection technique.

OBSERVATION

In some discussions of research methods there is a tendency to assume that observation is a technique only used by action theorists in their research into the meaningful construction of social life. This is not so; this section is about structural theorists' use of observation to generate empirical evidence of social forces. As in the case of the experiment, there is clearly a size limit involved – only in small-scale settings can an observer hope to be able to get sufficient evidence to properly judge structural hypotheses – but this does not mean that it *can't* be done.

Observation for positivist purposes has been most influentially carried out by anthropologists. Until relatively recently, anthropology has been largely functionalist in theoretical character, and its subject matter has typically been small-scale, face-to-face community life, particularly among tribal peoples. Participant observation – observation by joining in the lives of subjects – was established as an indispensable anthropological technique by the first fully-fledged anthropological

129

fieldworker, Bronislaw Malinowski. When war broke out in 1914, Malinowski was on his way to Australia. As an Austrian citizen he was technically an alien, and liable to be interned. He avoided this by persuading the Australian authorities to allow him to spend the duration of the war on the Trobriand Islands. Quite by chance, therefore, the first long-term use of participant observation in anthropology took place. Since then, Malinowski's fieldwork has become the model for anthropological research.

Nearer to home, a similar use of observation has been characteristic of 'community studies'. In both the USA and the UK these have usually been long-term studies of small communities, carried out along anthropological lines. The choice of locations for this kind of research shows how difficult it is to use observation on its own to reveal social structures in any but small-scale and static settings. These are nearly always rural communities, though it has been used in larger settings, alongside other techniques, in both the UK and the USA. The studies at Banbury in Oxfordshire, and community studies by Lloyd Warner in the USA, are good examples.

Elsewhere in structural sociology, participant observation on its own has tended to be used only in settings more or less equivalent to the small community – for example, the work-group (as in Tom Lupton's *On the Shop Floor* [1963] and Huw Beynon's *Working for Ford* [1973]), or the gang (as in William Foote Whyte's *Street Corner Society* [1943]).

Though these are by no means recent examples, they nonetheless demonstrate that it is an over-simplification to see observation as a purely ethnographic, descriptive instrument, usable only by action sociology. If action sociology had had a monopoly over the use of participant observation, social anthropology, for so many years an exclusively functionalist enterprise, would never have been born.

*Problems with observation for positivist purposes*

For the positivist researcher, the problem is how to retain *objectivity* and *distance* from the subject, so that the truth about structural forces can be acquired. Here, observation is not designed to help you see the world as the actors do; observation is used to get *your* (expert) theory of the structural world of the actors *right*. The positivist observer, therefore, has to make two kinds of decisions:

(1) Whether to risk objectivity by participating in the lives of the actors, or whether to remain in a detached, non-participant role;
(2) Whether to risk changing the behaviour of the actors by letting them know they are being observed, or to keep the research hidden from them.

Four possible options are thus available:
(1) Non-participant, covert observation
(2) Participant, covert observation
(3) Non-participant, overt observation
(4) Participant, overt observation.

Each of these options has particular problems associated with it:

| | | |
|---|---|---|
| Covert research | (1) and (2) | raises *ethical* dilemmas for the researcher |
| Overt research | (3) and (4) | creates the danger of the *observer effect* |
| Participatory research | (2) and (4) | creates dangers for the *internal validity* and *external validity* of the eventual account. |

*Internal validity*: participating in social settings means the observer is playing a role of one kind or another. While doing this may make his or her presence more acceptable to the actors, the danger is that the observer will only see things from his or her particular role-player's point of view. This means that the *internal* structure of the setting may not be properly identified; this is why the danger is described as being to the 'internal validity' of the account.

*External validity* is threatened by the very act of choosing one social setting in which to join and observe. Positivist participant observers want to gain evidence of social structural forces which apply to all similar social settings. The problem is therefore one of representativeness; how can the participant observer be sure that the example he or she has chosen *is* representative? Another big problem with observation for positivist purposes concerns numbers. When the number of people in whom you are interested is too large to observe, you must collect evidence to test your hypotheses some other way.

THE SURVEY

Almost always this is done by asking questions. Instead of observing people directly, a *survey* asks subjects to report on their lives for you – or, at least, on those aspects in which you are interested. The idea is to collect together all the answers of the people surveyed, convert these into quantities (statistics) and then analyse the answers to discover any significant, causal relationships. This is called *multi-variate analysis*.

For example, suppose you are carrying out research into voting behaviour. As part of this research, you hypothesise that there is a causal relationship between gender and voting behaviour. In your survey you ask your subjects how they voted in previous elections. Once you have collected together the answers, you can measure support for your hypothesis. You will know that A per cent of men voted Tory, B per cent Labour and C per cent Liberal Democrat; whereas X per cent of women voted Tory, Y per cent Labour and Z per cent Liberal Democrat. You can then judge whether your figures show that there is a significant relationship between gender and voting – provided you have controlled other possible variables.

But even if there is, you must then decide if it is a *causal* relationship. For example, it may be that you find more women than men vote Tory. But is this *because* they are women? Or is it for some other reason? For example, is it because more women than men do non-industrial jobs, and it is their job experience which is the causal factor? As we said earlier, there are always alternative hypotheses to be judged. The only way to decide which one should be supported is to test them all against the evidence. If, having tested the hypothesis that there is a relationship between occupation and voting, we find that it is stronger than the relationship between gender and voting, we may feel that *this* is the explanation we should support.

As in all science, the job of the researcher is to examine all possible explanations (alternative hypotheses) against the evidence, in order to *demonstrate* their relative strengths. This is why this research is called multi-variate analysis. It is the analysis of the relationship between a multiplicity of variables. The point is that the choice of an explanation is not made on a whim, but in the light of the evidence.

The results of multi-variate analysis in positivist sociology take a form familiar in all scientific research. Tables, graphs, histograms and so on, are all routinely used as pictorial images, measuring the extent of causal relationships.

Sometimes the evidence which we wish to analyse in order to test hypotheses is already available in statistical form. Such *official statistics* are the statistics collected by various agencies – governmental, commercial and charitable – for their purposes, but which can be used by social scientists to test hypotheses. The Census, carried out every ten years, is always a good source of basic data about Britain's population as a whole. In addition, there is a whole range of statistics about various categories within the population which can usefully be used for positivist purposes. Criminal statistics, health statistics, educational statistics, divorce statistics and others can all be manipulated in order to assess the plausibility of alternative hypothetical explanations.

In most cases, however, there are no official records of the incidence of ideas and behaviour in which sociologists are interested. It is in these cases that surveys are carried out to provide evidence. But it should not be thought that all surveys are of the same type. Some are designed to produce easily analysable data, and some are not.

*Forms of survey*

As we said earlier, the ease with which statistical analysis of answers to survey questions can take place depends upon the structure of the survey. Some surveys are carried out using printed questions on a *questionnaire*, usually sent by post. Obviously all the questions in a questionnaire are exactly the same for each *respondent*. That is, they are completely *structured*.

In an *interview*, which is the usual means by which surveys are carried out, the questions are often structured (asked in exactly the same way for each respondent), too. Structured questions are either closed-ended or open-ended. In closed-ended questions, respondents' answers are categorised from a range of alternatives provided, as in this example:

**Q** If there were a general election tomorrow who would you vote for?

Conservative
Labour
Liberal Democrat
Alliance
Nationalist
Other (state) ...........................................................................................................

Don't know
Too young to vote
Would not vote
(Refused Information)

In open-ended questions, respondents answer in any way they like. Open-ended replies in interviews are recorded verbatim. For example:

**Q** When you hear someone described as 'upper class', what sort of person do you think of?
　　*probe*: What other sorts of people do you think of as upper class?
　　*record fully.*

Closed-ended questions allow *pre-coding*. This means that a code is attached to each possible answer to a question. The interviewer rings the appropriate answer(s) and a respondent's closed-ended responses can be easily transferred into a computer. This allows easy multi-variate analysis. For example:

Q How is it that people come to belong to the class that they do?

|  | | |
|---|---|---|
|  | Born into it/inheritance/family | 01 |
|  | Innate ability | 02 |
|  | Hard work/achievement | 03 |
| *code all* | Work/job/position | 04 |
| *that apply* | Education | 06 |
|  | Income/standard of living | 06 |
|  | Possessions (e.g. home ownership) | 07 |
|  | Other (Specify)........................................................08 | |

*Source:* Rose, D., Marshall, G., Newby, H. and Vogler, C. 1984: The British questionnaire: the international project on class structure and class consciousness. British project, technical paper 3. University of Essex, Dept. of Sociology.

Such structured questions do not allow respondents to answer in a very meaningful or elaborate way, however. If an understanding of a respondent in greater depth is considered to be more important than easy statistical analysis, then a focused or unstructured interview may be used instead. A focused interview is centred around particular topics, but there is no structure to the individual questions, and no restrictions on how deeply a topic might be investigated.

An unstructured interview is really no more than a guided conversation, and is sometimes used by positivists for exploratory purposes. Where the researcher does not have enough information about the subject matter, it will not be possible to write a structured schedule or questionnaire designed to test specific hypotheses. A few unstructured interviews with well-placed and informative respondents is often the best way of acquiring enough knowledge to be able to devise a questionnaire, and to conduct a structured survey.

There is another reason why less than fully structured interviews are used. Structured interviews do not allow a full exploration of attitudes and ideas. Though open-ended questions can do the job to an extent, the most in-depth way of examining ideas, rather than behaviour, is by using an unstructured interview.

Herein lies the basic dilemma for the survey researcher. The more structured the technique, the easier the results can be analysed statistically. The more unstructured the technique, the greater the likelihood of in-depth understanding, particularly of ideas and attitudes. These choices can be portrayed like this:

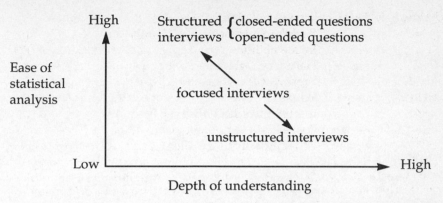

High

Structured {closed-ended questions
interviews {open-ended questions

Ease of
statistical
analysis

focused interviews

unstructured interviews

Low

High

Depth of understanding

## SAMPLING

Another factor also influences the kind of survey conducted. The point of a survey is to compare the results. Often the population about whom you want to make general statements is extremely large. It could be the whole of a country, all the inhabitants of a town, all the consumers of a particular product, all television-watchers, or whatever. In such circumstances it is clearly impossible to ask questions of everyone in whom you are interested. What is needed is a *sample* of respondents which is *representative* of the whole population. In many circumstances, even this sample will need to be fairly sizeable to ensure representativeness. This too, will tend to encourage the use of structured interviews. Since they take less time than unstructured ones, you can do more of them.

## FORMS OF SAMPLING

A *simple random sample* is one in which everyone in the population has an equal chance of inclusion. How the sample is drawn ensures randomness. Picking the required number of names out of a revolving drum is acceptable. Choosing everyone whose surname begins with the letter J is not.

A *stratified random sample* is one in which a random sample is drawn from within different categories of people in the population. This technique can be used if you think that a simple random sample will not guarantee the inclusion of sufficient numbers of kinds of people about whom you want evidence. For example, every fiftieth name on an electoral register, in a town whose population aged over eighteen is ten thousand or more, might well not include enough members of political or religious minorities, old-age pensioners or immigrants. However, drawing random samples from within each of the segments of the population in which you are interested will solve this problem.

*A quota sample* is the technique often used by market researchers and newspaper and television pollsters. This involves giving each interviewer a quota from within pre-selected categories of people – X females, Y males, Z old people and so forth, depending on their relative proportion in the overall population – leaving the interviewer to decide how and with whom to meet these quotas.

The purpose of all sampling is to ensure *representativeness* by eliminating *bias*. The people you interview must accurately represent the bulk of the population you do not interview. An over-representation of one kind of person means that the results will be biased in favour of the characteristics of this kind of person.

To eliminate bias, certain precautions are usually taken by sample survey researchers:

(1) The list of the whole population from which the sample is to be drawn (the *sampling frame*) must be accurate.

(2) The size of the sample (the *sample fraction*) must be sufficient; the larger the fraction, the more accurately it can represent the whole.

(3) The conduct of the survey must proceed properly. Only selected respondents should be interviewed. If, at the first attempt to locate someone, he or she is unavailable, you should *not* interview the spouse or the man next door who is mowing the lawn instead. At least three attempts at contact should be made. Only then is a substitute interviewed; ideally this person should be taken from a sample of the same size, held in reserve for this purpose. A certain amount of non-response is inevitable – people die, move house, go on holiday, refuse to be interviewed and so on. Non-response in postal questionnaire surveys is always higher than in interview surveys.

Interviews should take place over as short a period as possible, so that the survey is a snapshot of the population. Dragging interviews out can mean the passage of time may affect the result of the survey; for example, it is usually illegitimate to compare the results of questions asked with a three-month gap between them.

Assuming all these precautions against bias are taken, the positivist sociologist argues that the sample survey is an indispensable instrument of data collection for a scientific sociology. This is because it allows a carefully chosen minority to represent the whole, and because the results of the survey can be analysed with as much rigour as the natural scientist is able to muster in a laboratory experiment.

## INTERPRETIVE SOCIOLOGY

Action theorists – *anti-positivist*, interpretive researchers – see things very differently. Positivist sociologists argue that science must be used to explain social life because of the similarity they see between nature and society. It is because action theorists argue the opposite – that social life is nothing like nature – that they insist sociology should abandon any attempt to be scientific in this way.

### *Ontology*

For action theorists, the behaviour of human beings is not determined, as positivism suggests. It is the product of how people interpret the world around them. Appropriate behaviour is chosen in the light of how people define the situations they encounter – what they take social settings to *mean*.

### *Epistemology*

The topic shifts from the positivist interest in empirically validating *observer* theories, to an interest in understanding *actors'* theories. The perceptions and explanations of reality held by the participants in social situations, far from being irrelevant, now become the object of sociological interest. According to the action theorist, because behaviour originates in actors' interpretations of reality, sociological research should be concerned with gaining an *understanding* of these interpretations.

### *Methodology*

This can only be done by taking advantage of being human, putting yourself in the place of the actors, and working out how their theories, or interpretations, were arrived at. This is the process called *Verstehen*.

This is very different from objectively testing hypotheses against empirical evidence. For action theorists, sociology should be *non-scientific – anti-positivist*. Action sociology's subject-matter – the meanings behind people's actions – is *non-empirical*. The researcher, far from being objective, should be as *subjective* as possible. Natural scientists do not have to *be* daffodils, rocks, fish or atoms to arrive at cause and effect explanations about such phenomena, based on empirical evidence. Indeed, the only way 'true' explanations can be arrived at in natural science is by keeping as distant from your subject matter as possible. This is what objectivity means.

For action theorists, however, it is only *because* we are part of our subject matter – because we, too, are human – that we have any chance at all of understanding the reasons for our subjects' actions.

From this point of view, undertaking sociological research is not so different from being a social actor living in the world. All interaction between humans involves 'putting oneself in the place of the other'. That is, to live with, and interact with, one another, we all have to employ *Verstehen* all the time. To know how to *react* to someone's actions, we have to *understand* these actions.

Thus, in contrast to the positivist aim of *measurement* involving the collection of *quantitative* data, the anti-positivist aim is to *understand*, and involves the collection of *qualitative*, or *ethnographic* data. We will look at symbolic interactionist and ethnomethodological methods separately; whereas *verstehen* is the principal interpretive technique of the interactionist researcher, its use is a topic for ethnomethodologists.


## METHODS IN ANTI-POSITIVIST SOCIOLOGY

### SYMBOLIC INTERACTIONISM: USING *VERSTEHEN*

### *The interview*

All interpretation involves making sense of things – deciding they 'mean' something or other. As we said in Chapter 1, though we use dress, gesture, touch and even smell to communicate meaning, the most sophisticated way in which we do so is through language. For this reason interactionist research is typically very interested in what people say. What they say stands for what they mean – what the interactionist is interested in.

Obviously, talking can take place in an interview. But unlike the positivist use of the interview, the point is not to gain evidence of specific ideas and activities that we have decided *we* want to investigate. It is to explore the way our subject matter sees the world. Unlike the positivist, we want no preconceived ideas, and no leading questions. We do not want our actors to go where *we* lead them. We want to go where *they* lead *us*. If interviewing is used in interactionist research, it is almost always as unstructured as possible.

*Problems with the interview*

For many interactionists, however, even unstructured talking between sociologist and subjects does not avoid the danger they think is always present in question-asking of any kind. This is the equivalent of the 'observer effect' in observation. The interactionist argument is this. Just as the presence of the observer in observation may influence the behaviour of the actors, so the presence of the interviewer in interviewing may influence what the subject says. This is an *interviewer effect*.

In recent years both social psychologists and sociologists have produced evidence demonstrating that respondents tend to give answers to questions about their behaviour and beliefs not because these answers are the 'truth', but because *these are the answers they want the questioner to hear*. Why should this be? Sometimes it is easily understood. It is a bit much to expect undetected child-molesters and mass-murderers to reveal these aspects of their lives to complete strangers carrying out a research interview. But many interactionists have argued that there is a much more general interviewer effect to be aware of than this. Indeed, they say, we should expect a lack of candour to be normal in *all* interviewing.

Their argument is based on acknowledging the existence of what their theoretical position assumes is an inevitable part of every piece of social interaction. We described it like this in Chapter 6 (page 85):

Since we soon come to learn that others will interpret our behaviour, our *own* interpretive abilities allow us to manipulate these interpretations to suit our vision of ourselves.

We use our capacity to be *self-reflexive* in order to present the person we wish others to think we are. We play roles in a *creative* way to elicit from others the responses we desire. In effect, we manage, or orchestrate, the responses of others by presenting the image of our self we wish them to hold.

We become actors on the stage of life, writing our own lines.

If this *is* a part of every piece of social interaction, as the interactionist argues, we should hardly expect it not to happen in a piece of interaction which we call an interview. Indeed, since interviews are usually conducted between complete strangers, such 'impression management', as Goffman terms it, is probably more likely than in interaction between acquaintances. That is, we should *expect* the answers to our questions to be those our respondents want us to hear. Furthermore, what they want us to hear will be the result of their interpretation of us – what kind of person they have decided we are.

Though sometimes people want us to think bad things about them and deliberately set out to offend us, it is more usual for people to structure their behaviour to seek our approval. This view is supported by the evidence from research into research interviews. This shows that one of the most common sources of distortion in interview research is what is sometimes called the 'desirability effect'. Here a respondent's replies are those he or she thinks the interviewer will approve of. In effect, a desire to be thought well of outweighs any impulse to tell the truth.

For many interactionists, this problem is inherent in all kinds of interviewing as a source of data; it is not only a damning indictment of the more structured, question-asking techniques used in survey research, but it also makes *any* interview – however informal – likely to be a source of distortion rather than revelation.

For this reason, much interactionist research has abandoned deliberate question-asking as a data-collection technique. Instead, such researchers have taken *Verstehen* to its logical conclusion. To understand the meanings which underpin the actions of someone else, you become as much like that person as possible. To understand the actor's view of the world, you become that actor as far as you can.

*Participant observation/ethnography*

This is why interactionists use participant observation. Unlike positivists, such as anthropologists, who use the technique to reveal the structural forces determining behaviour and belief, the anti-positivist purpose is to use it to experience reality as the subject experiences it. The following accounts of the rationale behind the use of participant observation in two well-known interactionist studies – Howard Becker's of life in a medical school, *Boys in White* (1963), and Erving Goffman's famous study of life in a mental hospital contained in *Asylums* (1968) – clearly show how the interactionist's desire to understand the actors' view of the world demands the participation of the researcher in their lives. Becker (1968) writes:

> My immediate object in doing fieldwork at St Elizabeth's was to try to learn about the social world of the hospital inmate, as this world is subjectively experienced by him. I started out in the role of an assistant to the athletic director, when pressed, avowing to be a student of recreation and community life, and I passed the day with patients avoiding sociable contact with the staff and the carrying of a key. I did not sleep in the wards, and the top hospital management

knew what my aims were.

It was then and still is my belief that any group of persons – prisoners, primitives, pilots or patients – develop a life of their own that becomes meaningful, reasonable, and normal once you get close to it, and that a good way to learn about any of these worlds is to submit oneself in the company of the members to the daily round of petty contingencies to which they are subject.

Again, Becker (1970) writes:

The participant observer gathers data by participating in the daily life of the group or organisation he studies. He watches the people he is studying to see what situations they ordinarily meet and how they behave in them. He enters into conversation with some or all of the participants in these situations and discovers their interpretations of the events he has observed.

. . . in studying a medical school. We went to lectures with students taking their first two years of basic science and frequented the laboratories in which they spend most of their time, watching them and engaging in casual conversation. . . . We followed these students to their fraternity houses and sat around while they discussed their school experiences. We accompanied students in the clinical years on rounds with attending physicians, watched them examine patients on the wards and in the clinics, sat in on discussion groups and oral exams. We ate with the students and took night calls with them. We pursued interns and residents through their crowded schedules of teaching and medical work. We stayed with one small group of students on each service for periods ranging from a week to two months, spending many full days with them . . .

Here, then, is a thoroughly *anti-positivist* emphasis in sociological investigation. It is far removed from a concern with *non-involvement* in order to remain objective and develop an exclusive reliance on empirical evidence. The interactionist preoccupation is with as much involvement as possible, and an exclusive pursuit of the understanding of a *non-empirical* subject matter – actors' meanings.

This is done simply by being human. Only by taking advantage of being human yourself can you put yourself in the place of the actor in whom you are interested, and arrive at an understanding of how interpretation gives rise to action in social life.

From this discussion so far, it would seem reasonable to expect interactionists to rely exclusively on participant observation, with (at the very most) the occasional addition of informal question-asking in unstructured conversation. But to do this would leave interactionists with a problem. Being fully immersed in the world of their actors, they only finish the job when satisfied they have properly understood, as Goffman describes it, the 'tissue and fabric of social life'. But how do they persuade *others* they have done so? How do action theorists *prove* they have got the subjective experiences of others correct? Although Weber, the father of *Verstehen*, argued that empathy was sufficient – you 'do not need to be Caesar to understand Caesar', as he put it – the desire for proof, to *demonstrate* the validity of their understanding to others who were not there, has sometimes led even the most theoretically committed interactionists to use methods and data more usually associated with positivist research. In his celebrated observational study of homosexual activity in public conveniences, called *Tea Room Trade*, Laud Humphreys decided to leave nothing to chance in his efforts to persuade us of the truth of his portrayal. After his two-year-long lavatorial stint, he attempted to back up his findings by a sample survey of a hundred tea-room activists he had observed. (He constructed his sampling frame from car registration numbers.) Even Howard Becker, in *Boys in White*, produces quantified data to add 'scientific' weight to his observational account.

Among interpretivists, only ethnomethodologists are not faced with this problem of proof. This is why.

## *Ethnomethodology: investigating* verstehen

The ethnomethodological view is that 'doing sociological research' is no more and no less than another example of the accomplishment of social life by some members of the social world. That is, members using common-sense knowledge to understand, and therefore interact with, other members, and sociologists using sociological theories to understand actors' meanings, are engaging in exactly the same kind of social accomplishment. But in neither case can the understanding of the parties to a piece of interaction, whether sociologists or non-sociologists, be said to be 'true', or even necessarily what others might also have understood in the same setting. Understanding is only ever the result of *one* person's ability to make sense of *one* particular social situation. It cannot be disentangled from the situation itself, nor from the communicative equipment used by participants to make sense of it.

Ethnomethodologically, therefore, 'objective' truth is unobtainable because it does not exist. We have to abandon any search for 'explanations' of social situations which can be 'proved'. Though, like any other members of society, we can and do arrive at explanations of all the social situations in which we are involved (whether these are part of sociological research or not), these can only ever be *our* explanations, the product of *our* interpretive efforts.

This is why ethnomethodologists, as we saw in Chapter 6, wish to change the focus and interest of the sociological enterprise. Hamstrung by their membership of the social world, they believe sociologists can never provide proven explanations of the causes of social phenomena. However, they *can* reveal the procedures and methods by which humans make sense of the settings in which they find themselves. Indeed, since sociological research is another example of precisely this activity, the research act itself can be used as data. Though sociologists can never arrive at anything other than a subjective explanation of social life, this does not mean they cannot describe *how* they arrived at this view. In short, instead of *Verstehen* being the *instrument* sociology uses to understand and explain actors' meanings, it becomes the *topic* – the object of research – whether used by sociologists or non-sociologists.

How does ethnomethodology go about revealing the methods humans employ to understand each other? Its practitioners disagree among themselves about how this can be done.

## The experiment

As we saw in Chapter 6, in the typical ethnomethodological experiment, members' common-sense expectations of the behaviour of others are deliberately confounded, in order to demonstrate the kinds of mechanisms humans rely on to make sense of the settings in which they find themselves. In another well-known Garfinkel experiment (1967), for example, students were instructed to pretend that they were lodgers in their own homes. Faced with their close relations behaving as strangers, Garfinkel suggests that the rest of the family reacted oddly in each case because they had been deprived of one of the essentials for a social existence – the expectation that others will reaffirm that the world is what you take it as being. Even a very temporary reluctance to join in this ever-present task of confirming the 'facts' of existence – in this case, spending 15 minutes refusing to act in ways which would confirm family membership – is bound to produce bafflement and distress for the other participants in the situation.

## Participant observation/ethnography

Other ethnomethodologists argue for the benefits of descriptions, or 'ethnographies' as they call them, of the methods humans employ to make sense of social settings based on observation. These often relate to the most mundane, taken-for-granted activities. *Notes on the Art of Walking* is the name of one such well-known account. The idea is to show that even in demonstrating competence in abilities we take for granted, the human being is working at a social accomplishment of a complex kind.

## Conversational analysis

In so far as language is the principal method which humans employ to construct their social worlds, the description of how this method is employed is inevitably a central ethnomethodological interest. This is known as 'conversational analysis'. Harvey Sacks' well-known study of suicide (1967) is a good example of this route to 'members' methods'. It also demonstrates how ethnomethodological accounts of social activities bear little or no resemblance to accounts of the same activities from any other theoretical perspective.

In his research, Sacks is not really interested in suicide at all. As in other ethnomethodological studies, the particular activities under scrutiny are only useful as areas in which the real topic – how social life is accomplished – can be revealed.

Sacks carried out his research by examining transcripts of recorded telephone conversations between potential suicides and staff at a suicide prevention centre. The telephone calls are efforts on the part of the callers to communicate their desperation to the staff at the centre. For Sacks they are demonstrations of how:

(a) the callers and the staff members came to an understanding of each other;
(b) Sacks himself has to engage in just the same kind of sense-making methods in order to understand the meanings of the transcripts.

## THE RELATIONSHIP BETWEEN THEORY AND METHOD IN POSITIVIST AND INTERPRETIVE RESEARCH: AN ILLUSTRATION

J. MAXWELL ATKINSON: CORONERS AND THE CATEGORISATION OF DEATHS AS SUICIDES – CHANGES IN PERSPECTIVE AS FEATURES OF THE RESEARCH PROCESS

During the course of his research into suicide, Atkinson shifted his theoretical position completely. By using some of Atkinson's own story of his theoretical development, and by identifying the kinds of influences on this development, we can shed some light on the relationship between theory and method in sociology, and on the differences in positivist and anti-positivist sociological research procedures.

*Stage 1: positivism*

At the beginning of his research, Atkinson was concerned to discover the structural causes of suicide, so he engaged in ordinary positivist research. As we have seen, most positivist research involves the analysis of statistics collected by means of social surveys. The study of suicide, however, obviously demands the employment of rather different routes to such empirical evidence. In one of the earliest, and still famous studies of the subject, Emile Durkheim used official suicide statistics for the years 1866–78.

DURKHEIM'S 'SUICIDE'

From an examination of these statistics, three conclusions were immediately apparent to him:
(1) Within single societies the rate of suicide remains remarkably constant.
(2) The rate varies between societies.
(3) The rate varies between different groups within the *same* society.

According to Durkheim (1970), the only possible conclusion to be deduced from this is that suicide has structural origins. That is, variations in the suicide rate reflect different structural influences on the members of different societies, and on different groups within the same society.

Having been led to this general conclusion by an examination of the statistics, Durkheim constructed a more detailed hypothesis of the way in which suicide is structurally determined. This hypothesis explains which social groups have higher suicide rates than others. He argues that the rate of suicide among different groups or societies depends upon their degree of 'social integration' and 'moral regulation'.

By 'social integration' Durkheim refers to the degree to which values, attitudes, beliefs and patterns of behaviour are shared among members of a social group. By 'moral regulation' he means the way in which society controls the desires of individuals through socialisation; that is, the way in which norms and values constrain people's behaviour.

Having defined his concepts, Durkheim then hypothesised that 'suicide varies . . . with the degree of integration of the social group of which the individual forms a part', and set out to examine its empirical validity. He did this by means of a detailed scientific examination of the suicide statistics, according to the canons of scientific enquiry.

As a laboratory scientist would, Durkheim measured the relationship between what he hypothesised as causal or *independent* variables – the degree of integration and moral regulation of a social group – and the variable he believed was affected by this factor – the *dependent* variable – the rate of suicide in the group.

He examined this relationship in a range of groups included in the statistics: family, religious, political and occupational groups, groups at different times in a society's history, and groups in different societies, at different times in history. Cuff *et al.* (1979) described part of this multivariate analysis as follows:

> Durkheim starts by studying the publicly available information, the official statistics, on the rate of suicide for various countries in Europe. He notes that suicide is much more common in Protestant countries than in Catholic countries. In trying to establish the extent to which religious persuasion is linked with suicidal tendencies, Durkheim's problem resembles that of the researcher in the laboratory: how to control the conditions. In the above example, it could be that being Protestant is causally linked to a tendency to commit suicide, but it could also be that being German is the real determining agent. What Durkheim does is to hold nationality constant. He controls for the influence of the variable 'nationality' by comparing the influence of the two religions within a single society. For example, he finds that Bavaria has the fewest suicides of all the states of Germany, and it also has the most Catholics. He goes on to strengthen the empirical support for the link by showing that if we compare the provinces within Bavaria, we find that suicides are in direct proportion to the number of Protestants and in inverse proportion to the number of Catholics. In other words, where there are more Catholics there is less suicide, and where there are more Protestants there is more suicide.
>
> Durkheim has by no means proved that being Protestant and the tendency to commit suicide are definitely causally linked. The more times he demonstrates, however, that these two variables 'go together' in different situations, and the more he eliminates third variables (for example, 'nationality' (German), 'region' (Bavaria)), the more empirical support he provides for inferring a causal link.

Having completed his analysis, Durkheim was satisfied that his hypothesis had been proved correct. He concluded that suicide could be classified into three types, caused either by (a) under-integration into the group; (b) over-integration into it; or (c) too little moral regulation.

He called suicide in (a), from under-integration, *egoistic* suicide; suicide in (b) from over-integration, *altruistic* suicide; and suicide in (c), from too little moral regulation, *anomic* suicide.

## Egoistic suicide

Too little integration into a group, according to Durkheim, is the reason why single, widowed or divorced people are more prone to suicide than married people, or why married people without children are more prone to suicide than married people with a family.

Again, according to Durkheim, this explains why Protestants are more prone to suicide than Catholics. He argues that Protestants are more often left to make personal and moral choices in their lives than Catholics, who belong to a faith which instructs and guides their actions to a far greater degree.

## Altruistic suicide

Here, according to Durkheim, people are more prone to suicide the *more* integrated into the group they are. One example is of the Hindu widow who throws herself onto the funeral pyre of her husband, so that she will not be a burden on her family now that she is alone. (This is known as 'suttee'.) Another is of soldiers who sacrifice themselves for their fellow soldiers, or for their country.

## Anomic suicide

According to Durkheim, this kind of suicide is likely to happen among people whose socialisation is suddenly no longer appropriate to the new circumstances in which they find themselves. Having learnt one particular type of normative or moral regulation, they no longer know how to behave when dramatic alterations in their lives render these rules irrelevant. This, says Durkheim, makes them prone to despair and suicide. He argues that this can happen at times of great economic disruption, during severe slumps or rapid booms.

In all these cases, so far as he is concerned, Durkheim has demonstrated the externality of the causes of suicide. The impulse to take their own lives lies not inside individuals, like some kind of purely psychological or biological phenomenon. Instead, it is influenced by the kind of group or society into which individuals are socialised, whose cultural or normative characteristics promote or encourage the activity.

Because this is the theoretical case, argues Durkheim (1970), only scientific methodological procedures – the testing of hypotheses against empirical evidence – can provide evidence. In his own words: 'the basic proposition that social facts are objective . . . finds a new and especially conclusive proof in statistics and above all, in the statistics of suicide.'

Durkheim's work has been criticised from within positivism. For example, it has been argued that he failed to recognise the over-riding importance of geographical location. This criticism suggests that some of the types of people Durkheim considered most vulnerable – those living alone, or of the Protestant faith – are also more likely to live in urban rather than rural areas, and it is this that is the decisive causal factor.

This kind of criticism does not conflict with the principle of the statistical analysis of suicide, but with the manner in which Durkheim carried it out. As he began his research, Atkinson, too (positivistically), accepted that though there were weaknesses in the detail of Durkheim's work, the general approach was right, and that it could be improved upon. As Atkinson (1977) put it: 'By focusing on the way in which suicide statistics were compiled . . . the hope was that better rates could be computed so that a more thorough test of Durkheim's theory could be carried out.'

## Stage 2: interactionism

As his work progressed, however, Atkinson began to shift theoretical and methodological ground, away from structuralist/positivist assumptions, and towards interactionism/anti-positivism. The interactionist critique of positivist approaches to suicide is usually associated with the work of J. D. Douglas (1967).

### DOUGLAS: THE SOCIAL MEANINGS OF SUICIDE

In his book, *The Social Meanings of Suicide*, Douglas argues that the 'objective' indicators which Durkheim uses as evidence of the external determinants of suicidal behaviour – the official statistics of the rate of suicides among different groups and societies – are in fact no such thing. For him, far from being *objective* social facts, these statistics are in reality (like all social phenomena) very much the product of the *subjective* interpretations of particular individuals. His argument runs along the following lines.

The way a death becomes a suicide is a complex interpretive process, involving particular definitions of situations by particular individuals. (We only have to recall the earlier example, in Chapter 1, of how two police officers might interpret the death of a car driver, to appreciate this.) Since this is so, Durkheim is quite wrong to see these statistics as somehow 'true' indicators of suicide rates which can be analysed scientifically as though they were unproblematic, objective 'facts'. All they can be taken as being are reflections on the *particular* subjective interpretations of unforseen or unusual deaths arrived at by *particular* people, especially those whose job it is to arrive at such definitions, such as police officers and coroners.

Research into suicide should therefore take a very different form from the positivist emphasis on empirical evidence insisted upon by Durkheim and, initially, by Atkinson. For interactionists, suicides only ever become suicides because of the labels attached to death by particular individuals. Therefore we are never going to know the 'facts' of the matter – whether any death actually *was* a suicide or not.

What we can find out about, however, are the reasons why certain deaths come to be *labelled* as suicides. We can discover how the definition of a death as self-inflicted is arrived at. And, ironically enough, Durkheim's 'objective' indicators of the 'true' rate of suicide – the official statistics – can also help us.

Deaths only become suicides, and therefore included in the statistics, as a result of a process of official labelling. Since this is so, social research into the subject should concern itself with how and why such labels become attached – how the statistics are compiled. This, of course, is not the construction of empirical evidence of *external social determinants* of behaviour. It is the analysis of a very *non-empirical* activity – the interpretive procedures routinely employed by people in order to make sense of unexpected death.

For the interactionist, then, though the evidence remains the same as that used by the positivist – the suicide rates – the topic changes, from an interest in the labelled to an interest in the labellers. As Atkinson (1977) says about his conversion to interactionism:

> The question of how some deaths get defined as suicide could remain as a central focus without being inconsistent with the ideas of the new perspective. Whereas originally it had been intended that the investigation would lead to more rigorous ways of doing Durkheimian positivism, it now came to be directed to questions about the different available definitions of suicidal situations and about the social meanings of suicide.

As a consequence of this change in subject-matter, Atkinson's methods changed, too, though rather slowly and painfully, and somewhat unintentionally. He explains it thus:

> The general change in orientation did not, however, provide any immediate solution to the problem of what kind of empirical research should now be done, which is probably one reason why parts of the positivist legacy survived for so long. Another might have had to do with the very obvious difficulties involved in using participant

observation to study suicidal phenomena. But I also retained doubts about the vagueness and apparent sloppiness which seemed to characterise some of the research strategies adopted by interactionists: a funny story here, an apt quote from a 'subject' there, a few extracts from a newspaper or television . . . This was very different from the ordered way in which survey research could be carried out, and it was not easy to make the decision to forget so many hard-learned principles and exchange them for so vaguely specified an alternative. I therefore began to try ways of organising the research which would be both 'systematic' and relevant to my new found interests. In examining press reports of suicide, for example, the newspaper would be held constant by looking at different issues of the same one over a fixed period of time. Coding was used to collect data from coroners' records, IBM cards were punched, and reasonably large samples were still considered a necessity.

While these various positivistic methods were being deployed in the pursuit of answers to interactionist questions, other 'qualitative' data were steadily and unknowingly being collected. I had obtained access to a coroner's records as a result of an offer from the Essex County Coroner . . . Taking advantage of such an offer obviously involved meetings, but on the several occasions when I had lengthy discussions with him neither of us was aware that a 'research interview' was taking place . . .

*Stage 3: ethnomethodology*

Ultimately, however, interactionism lost out to ethnomethodology. Atkinson began to believe that the 'truth' about suicide was unobtainable. Instead, as in all ethnomethodological research, the topic became the mechanisms and methods humans (sociologists and non-sociologists) use to make sense of each other, and thereby to construct social life.

This is how Atkinson (1977) describes his final conversion:

The transition to ethnomethodology was rather more painful than the earlier change of perspective. For not only did it involve discarding some of the most deeply entrenched traditional rationales for doing sociology (e.g. to construct decontextualised descriptions and theories of social action which are different from and better than the situated practical descriptions and theories of members), but in addition the new analytic interest was to be in the topic of descriptive procedures

| | POSITIVISM IN SCIENCE | POSITIVISM IN SOCIOLOGY | ANTI-POSITIVISM IN INTERPRETIVE SOCIOLOGY |
|---|---|---|---|
| **ONTOLOGY** | Nature an objective, *given* reality, made up of phenomena in invariable causal relations | Society is an objective, *given* reality – a *social structure* – whose existence is manifested in actors' ideas and actions | Society is the construction of its members. Social reality is made up of individual occasions of interaction accomplished by the actors involved because they are capable of: (i) interpretation (ii) meaningful action |
| **EPISTEMOLOGY** | Knowledge of the Laws of Nature only possible by the collection of demonstrable proof of their existence – by the collection of *empirical evidence*. (*Quantification* of the extent of relationships) | Knowledge of the impact of structural forces on actors' lives only possible by the collection of *empirical evidence* of regularities of thought and behaviour patterns: i.e. validation of *observer* theories via *quantification* – *statistical evidence* – of the extent of thought and behaviour patterns | Knowledge of interpretation and meaningful action only possible by acquiring an *understanding* of the ways actors see the world, and by acquiring an *understanding* of the meanings which underpin their actions: i.e. understanding of *actors'* theories via the acquisition of *qualitative* evidence |
| **METHODOLOGY** | The deduction of Hypotheses and the attempt to disprove them empirically: the *Hypothetico–Deductive method* — THEORY → HYPOTHESIS → TESTING → CONCLUSIONS → (cycle) | The deduction of Hypotheses and the attempt to disprove them empirically: the *Hypothetico–Deductive method* — THEORY → HYPOTHESIS → TESTING → CONCLUSIONS → (cycle) | The use of *Verstehen*: the researcher making use of the fact that he/she, like the actors who are the subject-matter, is a creative social actor, capable of interpretation: i.e. research = *self-conscious social interaction* |
| **METHOD** | *Experimentation* under controlled conditions, in order to measure the extent of any causal relationship between *Variables* | (1) *The Experiment:* *Problems:* practically difficult ethically problematic "observer effect" (2) *Observation:* e.g. Anthropology — Participant / Non-Participant — ROLES — Overt / Covert. *Problems:* limited scope – small-scale limits on objectivity of results: (a) "Observer effect" (b) Over-sympathy with subjects – ("going native") (c) Internal validity – the whole picture? (d) External validity – representativeness of case study (3) *The Survey:* (a) Types of questions (b) Choice of respondents (*Sampling*) (c) Problems of *Linterviewer effect*? (d) Multi-variate analysis | (1) *Symbolic Interactionist Research:* the *use of Verstehen* – everyday techniques of interaction – to understand and explain: (a) *Talk* e.g. *the interview* (b) *Participant Observation/Ethnography* e.g. Becker, Goffman, Humphreys. *Problems:* proof of understanding – Weber: "One does not have to be Caesar to understand Caesar." True? (2) *Ethnomethodological Research:* the description of how members use everyday techniques of interaction to understand each other and create social order – i.e. the *investigation of Verstehen*: (a) *The Experiment* e.g. Garfinkel (b) *Observation/Ethnography* (c) *Conversational Analysis* e.g. Sacks |

rather than in suicide *per se*. Data on suicidal phenomena thus became no more and no less appropriate than data on any other topic describable by members . . .

The main elements in the positivist-action debate are summarised in the table on page 151.

## SOCIOLOGY AND SCIENCE: FURTHER DEVELOPMENTS

From the 1970s onwards, the story of the relationship between sociology and science has developed in new ways. Developments so far can be summarised as follows:
(a) **Positivist science** argues that
  (i) nature consists of phenomena in cause-and-effect relationships, which are
  (ii) wholly capable of empirical revelation and measurement, and
  (iii) demonstrable in a completely value-free way.
(b) **Positivist sociology** argues that
  (i) though humans possess minds and therefore have ideas and theories, these non-empirical phenomena are *irrelevant* as influences on social life because
  (ii) societies consist of objective structural forces producing behaviour and belief which
  (iii) can be revealed and measured wholly empirically and
  (iv) in a completely value-free way.
(c) **Action theory**, in contrast, argues that
  (i) ideas and actors' theories are the *essence* of social life, and
  (ii) since these phenomena are non-empirical, and since positivist science requires proof by means of empirical evidence
  (iii) sociology cannot be a positivist science.

We must must now add two other elements to the plot.

(d) **Realist science** argues that:
  (i) no science is wholly empirical in method, so that
  (ii) although sociology has to concern itself with non-empirical phenomena, like actors' ideas and theories
  (iii) this does not mean that sociology cannot be a non-positivst, *realist*, science.
(e) **Sociologists and historians of science** influenced by the work of **T. S. Kuhn** argue that:

152

(i) positivism is wrong to claim that sciences are value-free since

(ii) *all* scientific work can be shown to be influenced by the exercise of human prejudice, preference and partisanship, and

(iii) since such judgements and choices are socially and historically generated and specific

(iv) *scientific* knowledge, like all forms of human knowledge, should be recognised as a social and historical product.

## THE ANTI-POSITIVISM OF REALIST SCIENCE: EXPLANATION AS WELL AS DESCRIPTION

For the positivist, science is concerned to reveal regularities in the causal relationships between observable things – to discover the extent to which something happens when something else has happened. For example, Boyle's law states that, given a constant temperature, when one thing happens – an increase in pressure – another thing (always) happens – a change in the volume of gas. The discovery of such causal relationships between observable phenomena is the goal of positivist science.

For the realist, however, the discovery of such observable relations, though necessary, is not sufficient. For example, to properly explain the relationship between air pressure and the volume of a gas we need to go beyond a description of this relationship: we also need to know *how gases work*. In effect, we need to know what it is about the constitution/make-up of gases that enables the change in pressure to have the observed effect it does. This knowledge – about the molecular structure of gases – is theoretical knowledge of structural features, hidden beneath what is directly observable to us.

Realists are therefore always concerned to understand the structures, mechanisms or processes that underpin observable events and enable causal relations to occur. Much of the time, however, such underlying structural features are not observable at all, contradicting the basic requirement of positivist science. As Cuff, Sharrock and Francis (1990) put it:

We can observe the regular pattern which is the maturation of the human organism, the growth from infant to adult, but we cannot observe in the same way the working of the genetic code embodied in DNA, although the genetic code is the mechanism producing the growth of the organism. The business of (realist) science involves, typically, the movement from the examination of the manifest, observably regular behaviour of phenomena to investigation into their deeper structures in order to discover how the structures act as 'mechanisms', that is, serve to make things work as they do.

A brief look at typical Marxist explanations demonstrates why realists often claim Marxist thinking represents realism in social-scientific practice. When observing a man cutting wheat in a field, overseen by someone else, a Marxist would argue that we can only make sense of such an action by knowing whether this is the labour of a slave, a tenant, or a wage-labourer. That is, it is only knowledge of modes of production, classes, and the relationship between the base and the superstructure that makes observable social life explicable. Such underlying structural features cannot be seen – they are theoretical entities – but to a Marxist they are still the reality that needs to be understood in order to make sense of what *can* be seen.

Again, Marxists wish us to realise the centrality of certain institutionalised relationships in capitalist society. Thus, we are asked to recognise, for example, the importance of the relationship between employer and employee, between landlord and tenant, between the board of directors of a firm and its shareholders, and so on. These relationships are observable when, for example, an employer hands over a wage packet to an employee, when a tenant pays a landlord rent, and when shareholders receive dividends. But according to Marxists, to *explain* such relationships we have to go beyond the observable and understand the structural context which makes them possible. Seeing an employer give a wage-packet to an employee only makes sense to Marxists because they know about underlying structural features in capitalist society – the existence of wage-labour, the relationship between classes, the pursuit of profit, and so forth. They make sense of what they see because they 'know' about the structure of capitalist society.

For realists, this is how all sciences work: rather than the mere description of observable regularities, an explanation by reference to non-observable phenoma is always necessary. Just because sociology has to deal with ideas and interpretations underpinning observable action, or with structural relations underlying these ideas and interpretations, it is not rendered non-scientific, as the positivist would argue; for realists, dealing with such underlying processes is simply what *all* sciences do.

## THE ANTI-POSITIVISM OF T. S. KUHN

In 1962 Thomas Kuhn, a historian of science, published a work called *The Structure of Scientific Revolutions* which has had a profound impact on the way science and scientific knowledge has since been understood. In effect, Kuhn argues against the positivist claim that science collects knowledge in a purely objective way, dealing only with facts and excluding judgements. His argument is that the production of scientific truth is always influenced by fashion and trend, by politics and the exercise of power, and by choices about what should be known about and what should not, just like any other form of human production. Since the attraction of science for the project of modernity has been its claim to be *unlike* other forms of knowledge, to deal *only* with facts, to provide *demonstrable* proof and to enable certain knowledge, Kuhn's argument represents a major assault on the scientific foundations upon which much modernist theorising has been built.

To understand Kuhn's ideas it will be useful to return to Weber's methodological writings to which we referred earlier (see pp. 70–1). According to Weber, the following features concerning the production of sociological knowledge must be remembered:

(1) Human beings can only select *aspects* of reality to know about: it is impossible for a human being to know *everything* about reality.
(2) This selection not only determines what topic is researched, i.e. what aspect of reality is chosen to be investigated. It also determines the questions that are chosen to be asked about this aspect of reality, i.e. the theoretical approach to be employed.
(3) The selection of topic and theory are inevitably based on the researcher's *values*, i.e. upon what he or she thinks is 'worthy of being known about' as Weber described it.
(4) Since these values are themselves characteristic of a society at a particular time in history, sociological knowledge is, therefore, not only a selection. It is also always a *social* product, generated out of the use of socially created value-judgements of 'worth 'and 'importance'.

Weber's 'debate with Marx' about the nature of capitalist society demonstrates his argument. Though both Weber and Marx agreed that knowing about capitalist society was a highly important and worthy project, the aspects of capitalism they each chose to explore reflected different theoretical interests.

As we have seen, Marx was interested in the role of economic forces in social change, and in the influence of the mode of production on the character of capitalist society. Weber was more interested in the role of ideas in social change and in the influence of the rationalisation process on the character of capitalist society. But, as we saw earlier, Weber does not claim to be 'right' and Marx 'wrong'. He and Marx have focused on just one part of capitalist reality; it is impossible to gain access to the whole. This, as we saw, leads Weber to use *ideal-types* in presenting his partial accounts of selected aspects of the world – to exaggerate the features of reality he is interested in, so that others can be left in no doubt where his preferences lie. In fact, his argument is that *all* knowledge is bound to be ideal-typical.

Though not claiming to, Kuhn in effect picks up this kind of argument about the nature of sociological knowledge and applies it to the process of producing natural knowledge in the natural and physical sciences. He claims that an examination of the history of these sciences shows how this sort of selection process *always* occurs – that scientists have to *choose* which phenomena to research, and to *choose* a theoretical approach to carry this research out. But, argues Kuhn, these choices are always made in social contexts; there are always *social* and *political* influences affecting how scientists do their work. He describes this by arguing that any scientific knowledge is produced from within a particular tradition, or *paradigm*, which determines what research is done and how it is carried out. Scientists belong to one of these traditions or another; scientific work always takes place from within one paradigm or another.

The history of a science is the history of the rise and fall of paradigms. For some periods of time only one paradigm prevails, and any ideas which threaten it are despatched away from the centre of the stage. In such times, scientific work takes the form referred to by Kuhn as 'normal science'; nearly all scientists work within the dominant paradigm, and different ways of looking at the world are treated with scorn. In this way, dominant paradigms exercise power and sustain dominance as 'dogma'.

Medicine provides a good contemporary example of such a state of affairs. Despite the wide range of therapies available – homeopathy, hypnotherapy, acupuncture, faith-healing, hydrotherapy and many others, the practice of Western medicine is dominated by one version of medical truth. The medical establishment (represented in Britain by the British Medical Authority, the BMA), funding bodies, research institutes and teaching hospitals, all practise and thereby reproduce one form of therapy; there is one *dominant* way of looking at illness (as organic in origin and treatable by physical intervention – by drugs or surgery for example). So, when you turn up at your doctor's surgery, you are not asked to make a *choice* from the array of alternative therapies in existence. You are obliged to have a consultation with a doctor trained in one particular way, to the exclusion of others. In Kuhn's terms, there is a dominant medical paradigm.

Things are changing in medicine, however. Whereas faith-healers and hypnotherapists used to be called 'quacks', they are now called 'alternative' or 'complementary' practitioners. Today, a British general practitioner (GP) is more likely to offer homeopathy or acupuncture as part of NHS treatment – a state of affairs which would have been unthinkable twenty years ago. The former 'fringe' medicines are slowly becoming more respectable; *their* version of what makes people ill, and how they should be treated, is gaining more and more legitimacy. In fact, we could be seeing the beginning of the demise of orthodox medicine as a dominant paradigm, and the emergence of a world where alternative versions of medical truth compete with each other on equal terms – for patients and funding and for legitimacy and authority. Kuhn describes how the fall from grace of a dominant paradigm in any science produces a time of ferment and uncertainty in the science – a time, as he describes it, of revolution.

As in all revolutions, old certainties are abandoned, competing versions of truth and virtue multiply, and confusion reigns. Peace and certainty can only break out again when a victor emerges from the conflict among those who would be king. However, this can only happen when the power of one of these pretenders becomes so great that its competitors are defeated; from its newly acquired position of dominance, the victorious paradigm can then begin to dictate the practice of the science, and 'knowledge' and 'progress' can race ahead once more. In effect, the emergence of a new dominant paradigm means the production of a new version of truth and certainty. According to Trigg (1985): 'Scientists once believed in a substance called phlogiston and now they do not. They once believed the atom could not be split, whereas now they continue to search for sub-atomic particles.'

Kuhn uses this famous drawing, which can be seen as either a duck or a rabbit, to illustrate how the world is seen differently after the destruction of an old dominant paradigm, and the emergence of a new one. Kuhn (1962) says: 'What were ducks in the scientific world before the revolution are rabbits afterwards.'

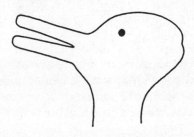

Why do scientists change their paradigms? Since the emergence of a prevailing paradigm is the result of social influences – through the practice of the politics of persuasion – we should expect such influences to be behind the decision of individual scientists to abandon previously held beliefs in favour of new ones. Kuhn (1962) says scientists choose a new paradigm 'for all sorts of reasons and usually several at once . . . Some of these reasons . . . depend upon idiosyncracies of autobiography and personality. Even the nationality or the prior reputation of the innovator and his teachers can sometimes play a significant role.'

So science, instead of being the steady, value-free accumulator of more and more evidence about reality, is in fact just what communities of believing scientists are led to do at a certain time in history, in a particular set of social circumstances. The dominance of one paradigm and the knowledge its practitioners purvey is not, therefore, caused by any monopoly over truth it may have, but because of its monopoly over *power* and, as a result, its means socially to control what *counts* as truth. The production of scientific knowledge is thus underpinned by choices, preferences and judgements not *freely* chosen by scientists, but orchestrated and reinforced by the political activity of a scientific establishment. Scientific knowledge is therefore not powerful because it is true; it is true because it is powerful.

The sociology of science – the investigation of the social and political origins of particular paradigmatic 'certainties' or 'truths' therefore becomes highly important. Trigg (1985) expressed it thus: 'Societies or traditions determine what we count as knowledge . . . what we believe or claim to know is merely the product of social forces of which we may be utterly ignorant . . .'

This can happen at both the structural and the interpretive level. At the level of structure, the institutional and ideological means by which scientific communities attempt to exercise political and social control over the production of knowledge in their name are of interest. At the level of action and interpretation, the construction of scientific knowledge as an outcome of meaningful interaction and negotiation in laboratory settings is of interest.

Following Kuhn's argument leads us back to the issue of *relativism* discussed in Chapter 7. This is made explicit in the arguments in support of Kuhn by the philosopher of science, Paul Feyerabend. According to Trigg (1985), Feyerabend:

> Considers that there is no more ultimate way of referring to reality than through the particular tradition we belong to. Instead of reality controlling our beliefs, at least to some extent, it seems as if the beliefs of a tradition determine what is to count as real. Within any one of

158

them, we can gain the illusion that knowledge can be and has been attained. Yet once we see that many conflicting traditions have the same conceit, we realize, it is alleged, that judgements of truth only have relative validity. They hold for our colleagues in the tradition to which we are attached, but not for those outside.

This is an anti-positivist epistemology diametrically opposed to that of the anti-positivism of realism in the last section. Here, as Trigg (1985) puts it:

'Reality' has no meaning apart from what is believed real by some group. The very concept of an objective world, independent of all points of view, has disappeared. Ontology has thus become dependent on epistemology. What there is is seen as the product of our strategies for finding things out. If our epistemology changes, as when we move from one worldview to another, so do our beliefs about what is real.

We shall shortly hear loud echoes of this claim from an unexpected location when we look at post-structuralist research into language and text (see pp. 168–71). This is part of the last chapter in this book, in which we look at some of the most recent developments in theorising and research practices in sociology.

# CHAPTER TEN

# *Recent developments in sociological theories and research practices*

The dispute between positivist and action theorists continued throughout the 1960s and into the early 1970s. During the second half of the 1970s and at the beginning of the 1980s systematic attempts were made to bring the conflict to an end, with important consequences for the relationship between theory and method.

## TRIANGULATION

The combining of theories and/or methods, though by no means a new idea, was pursued with a new vigour by researchers exasperated by the dogmatism and intolerance exhibited by the zealots on either side of the conflict. By the 1970s, for many sociologists, a renewal of interest in the activity of data collection and knowledge acquisition had become a crying need, as opposed to the prosecution of an increasingly sterile doctrinal debate. If this meant deliberately constructing projects to satisfy different schools of theoretical and methodological thought, they were happy to do so.

Two well-known studies typify this trend: Howard Newby's study of Suffolk agricultural workers, *The Deferential Worker* (1977), and Eileen Barker's study of the Moonies, *Making of a Moonie: Choice or Brainwashing?* (1986). Excerpts from their research memoirs show their determination to break with previous dogmatism; Newby by combining methods, and Barker by combining theories and methods.

*Howard Newby*

The methodology was deliberately eclectic, involving the routine perusal of agricultural and population census statistics, a search of

160

historical sources (both documentary and oral), participant observation and a survey investigation. Since many of the concerns of the study involve the inter-relationships of farmers and farmworkers and of farmworkers with each other, it was apparent from the outset that a degree of participant observation would be necessary. However, the almost complete lack of sociologically relevant data, even of a sociographic kind, made it desirable to conduct a survey. In effect, the survey and the period of participant observation increasingly came to complement each other: insights gained from participant observation could be checked against survey data; on the other hand much of this data could often only become meaningful through the experiences gained from living with a farmworker and his family in a tied cottage for six months and gaining first-hand knowledge about the work and community situation.

*Eileen Barker*

There is in sociology a time-honoured dichotomy between those schools that focus on interpretive understanding and those that stress more behaviourist, positivistic or scientific approaches. What was to be my approach? Should I perhaps become an ethnomethodologist and investigate the taken-for-granted Moonie world, or should I regard Moonies as rats and dispassionately watch them running about their mazes, dismissing from my mind any notions of meaning or conscious purpose that could not be covered by stimulus/response or the more sophisticated operant-conditioning models of behaviour? Or perhaps I should forget about individuals as such and search only for structures and functions at a societal level? Would I adopt a philosophical anthropology that assumed we are complicated but nonetheless determined, reacting robots: or are we free, initiating creators, capable of self-determination? Whom would I believe when it came to descriptions of the Unification Church? Who was more trustworthy, the brainwashed Moonies themselves or the sceptical critics? Would I learn more as an outsider or an insider? What was the true reality and how could I get to know about it? Was I to be guided by fact or theory or both? But then, which theory, and how was I to get the facts?

I began to realize that there could be no one answer. Several of the perspectives seemed to be necessary while none was sufficient for my purposes. I was convinced that without having a methodology as scientific as possible one would be unlikely to produce a sociological contribution that would add anything to all the claims and counterclaims which already existed. But it also seemed that without *Verstehen*, or in other words some kind of empathetic understanding, one could not hope to find one's data in the first – or in the last – place.

In the end I decided on three main lines of approach: in-depth interview, participant observation and questionnaire. From the interview I hoped to understand the individual as an individual. Just over thirty interviews were carried out on the basis of a random sample of the membership. They were tape-recorded and usually lasted for between five and nine hours. The longest lasted for twelve hours. From the participant observation (that is, from living in UC centres and attending various courses), I hoped to observe the interpersonal level, and from the questionnaire I hoped to see patterns and relationships that I might suspect existed but about which I could only generalize from a large number of respondents. All the British members and several European and American members were given a forty-one page questionnaire containing both 'open' and 'precoded' (closed-ended) questions . . . Added to these were over 100 responses to a similar questionnaire, filled in by a control group, that is by non-UC members who were similar in age and background (class, education and religion) to the UC membership. This was a methodological necessity if I were to be able to assess the extent to which the phenomena I was analysing was peculiar to the UC members . . . of course, all three methods shed light on the other aspects in which I was interested. I certainly could not have produced the questionnaire if I had not first spent two years conducting a large number of interviews, living with members and undergoing the so-called 'brain-washing' process. All of this was necessary for the formulation of hypotheses to be tested by the questionnaire and for learning the language in which the questions were to be couched. And, of course, I did learn much about individuals and their interactions from the questionnaire, just as during the participant observation, I could actually observe the individuals interacting with others, and I could try to judge the overlaps and differences between their presentation of self in an interview and in an actual social context.

## POLITICS AND FUNDING

By the 1980s, the appearance on the horizon of an enemy hostile to *any* version of sociology concentrated the minds of erstwhile opponents wonderfully, encouraging them to forget their doctrinal differences in order to present a unified front. Thatcherism stalked the land, with social sciences in general, and sociology in particular, in its sights. Deliberate attempts were made to undermine sociological work. The declaration that 'there is no such thing as society' by the Lady herself, gives a flavour of the individualistic ideology subscribed to by any 'one of us'. The ontological opposition was total; sociology seeks to explain individual life and advantage or disadvantage at least in part by seeing this originating in unequal social structures; for Thatcher, however, there are only individuals and their families, and we have only ourselves to congratulate for our successes or blame for our misfortunes. From such a viewpoint, social 'sciences' deal with fictitious subject-matter and their spurious claims to scientific status simply seek legitimacy for apologist pronouncements excusing individual culpability. Big guns were fired off at sociology; Sir Keith Joseph – then the Secretary of State for Education – forced the Social Science Research Council, responsible for funding social science research, to change its name to the Economic and Social Research Council and hired Lord Rothschild, an eminent academic, to carry out an inquiry into the subject. The idea was to expose sociology as left-wing gobbledegook once and for all, but Rothschild was too thorough and impartial to act as Thatchers's Lord High Executioner. Having implemented an inquiry they believed would endorse their own prejudices, the Thatcherites had to cool the onslaught when their own guided missile refused to fire.

However, real changes were wrought in sociology by this experience. In order to survive in the hard world dominated by Thatcherite values, many sociologists in Britain learned the need to be politically attractive and non-controversial. *Policy-oriented*, applied research, aiming at specific practical outcomes, appeared more and more often; the name of the game was survival, but to survive one needed funding, and to gain funding research had to be 'useful'.

Furthermore, since research funds became scarce, researchers became more inclined to choose *inexpensive* methods, rather than those they would have chosen had saving money not become a prime objective. In addition, university departments in all disciplines, including sociology, began to be judged on their research records with requests for funding being considered in the light of them. In such a competitive research climate, another non-theoretical reason for choosing research procedures became important; the *speed* at which research could be completed, published, and available for recognition. During the 1990s, it is likely that such competition will become more intense still; with polytechnics becoming universities and higher-education funding being unified, there has been strong support for the stratification of universities into

163

'teaching-only' and 'teaching-plus-research' institutions, with the bulk of research funding going to those successful in the research-ranking exercise. There is a likelihood that the bulk of research funding will therefore be concentrated in a limited number of 'centres of excellence'.

## STRUCTURATION

Anthony Giddens introduced the concept of *structuration* into sociological theory in a deliberate attempt to construct a theoretical synthesis between structural and action approaches.

Giddens' theory refers to the 'duality of structure'. Not only do structures constrain and determine certain forms of behaviour, they also *enable* behaviour; they provide opportunities, as well as limitations. Furthermore, the structural circumstances within which human action, or *'agency'* as Giddens calls it, takes place are thereby reproduced, or redefined, by this action. That is, while an action inevitably takes place within a structural context, this context in turn is regenerated, or transformed, by the action. There is thus a dialectical relation between structure and action. Bilton *et al.* (1987) explain it thus: 'On the one hand, "structures are constituted by action", yet, on the other hand, "action is constituted structurally". Such a logic seeks to overcome the positivist/anti-positivist split.'

As yet, relatively little research has genuinely attempted to apply structuration ideas to research practice; most attempts to go beyond the 'war' are triangulation efforts of the sort already mentioned, aiming to *combine* structure and action research in a project, rather than to aspire to a genuine *synthesis* of the two approaches. Probably still the best example of a true application of structuration ideas in research is Paul Willis' famous study *Learning to Labour* (1977).

*Learning to Labour* is a piece of research which tries to identify the structural and action features of the educational careers of a group of working-class boys – the 'lads' as they are known. In effect, Willis is interested in finding out why working-class youths end up in working-class jobs – why and how schooling teaches them to 'learn to be labourers'.

Willis takes an orthodox Marxist view of class and points to the disadvantages experienced by the boys as a result of their position in the class structure of a capitalist society. But he also reveals the ways in which the boys *choose* to conduct their lives *within* this structural context, demonstrating how they interpret the reality of their circumstances – how they theorise about their world – and take action they deem to be appropriate in the light of this theoretical knowledge, so far as their structural position allows them. They are thus not simply the passive recipients of structural forces – Willis is no Bowles and Gintis, seeing pupils as helpless pawns in a game played within education and refereed by capitalism. For the 'lads' *know* they are being badly served by the school and take consciously chosen action in order to express their resistance to the educational process. They refuse to have anything to do with schooling, enthusiastically embracing anti-school culture, and use the symbolic means available to them to express their defiance. They thus attempt to liberate themselves from the structural shackles of the school experience by using the cultural equipment of the working class – such as cigarettes and alcohol – not simply because smoking and drinking are against school rules, but because by such symbolic means they can join the adult working-class world. They see this as a haven to which they can aspire once they are away from the control of the educational system. Even though their resistance to education means they end up where the system wanted them all along – uneducated and therefore condemned to working lives as manual workers – Willis' point is that their journey to this status is not a structurally-created inevitability; it is *chosen* by the actors for their own reasons, in the light of *their* theories of their world. The fact that by these actions the structure of this world is reproduced does not minimise the importance of human agency in their story.

WILLIS' METHODS

Layder *et al.*'s (1991) analysis of the research implications of structuration is this: 'In Giddens' terms all strategic activity has an irreducible interpretive component and, as a consequence, all social research has an ethnographic aspect to it . . . As a result, all social research must be sensitive to the "complex skills" which actors display in their day-to-day activities . . . '

Since this is so, it is not surprising that Willis' work, commended by Giddens himself as an exemplar of structuration research, should employ the following research methods, described by Willis (1977):

The main study was of a group of twelve non-academic working-class lads [who] . . . were selected on the basis of friendship links and membership of some kind of an oppositional culture in a working-class school . . . The main group was studied intensively by means of observation and participant observation in class, around the school and during leisure activities; regular recorded group discussions; informal interviews and diaries. I attended all of the different subject classes and options (not as a teacher but as a member of the class) attended by the group at various times, and the complete run of careers' classes . . . I also taped long conversations with all the parents of the main group, and with all senior masters of the school, main junior teachers in contact with members of the group, and with the careers officers coming into the school . . . I followed all twelve boys from the main group . . . into work. Fifteen short periods of participant observation were devoted to actually working alongside each lad in his job, and were concluded with taped interviews with the individual and selected interviews with foremen, managers and shop stewards.

The relationship between his theoretical interests and methods is made plain by Willis (1973):

The qualitative methods and participant observation used in the research, and the ethnographic format of the presentation were dictated by the nature of my interest in 'the cultural'. These techniques are suited to record this level and have a sensitivity to meanings and values as well as an ability to represent and interpret symbolic calculations, practices and forms of cultural production. In particular the ethnographic account . . . can allow a degree of the activity, creativity and human agency within the object of study to come through into the analysis and the reader's experience.

## CULTURAL ANALYSIS

Willis' study is one of the most famous examples of a tradition of *cultural analysis* which began to be fashionable in Britain in the late 1970s and into the 1980s, much of it emanating from Birmingham University's Centre for Contemporary Cultural Studies (CCCS). The head of the centre at that time was Stuart Hall (now Professor of Sociology at the Open University). This sort of work, influenced by Frenchman Roland Barthes, encourages the use of *semiotics* – the study of signs – in social research in order to reveal the ways in which cultural artefacts can be pressed into service in social life to serve symbolic, or expressive ends – as forms of representation of meaning.

As we have just seen, interpretive method is at the heart of Wilis' work: he wants to understand how schooling appears to the 'lads' and how their theories of this process lead them to symbolically express resistance to it. Cultural analysis does not restrict itself to an examination of the *intentional* use of symbols by actors, however. The sociological use of semiotics also directs our attention to the *unconscious* construction of symbolic representations in social life, an understanding of which requires the insight of the semiologist in order to *decode* the signs.

For example, CCCS researchers into youth subcultures like Stuart Hall and Tony Jefferson (*Resistance through Ritual*, 1976), and Dick Hebdige (*Subculture: the Meaning of Style*, 1979) combine a Marxist perspective on social structure with a semiological interest in the symbols represented in forms of dress, music, ritual and language/discourse favoured by different kinds of working-class youth; the project is to reveal the meanings and order behind seemingly meaningless and disordered cultural practices. Tony Jefferson (1976) makes sense of teddy-boy subcultural style, dominant in the 1950s in Britain, as follows:

> Despite periodic unemployment, despite the unskilled jobs, Teds, in common with other teenagers at work during this period, were relatively affluent. Between 1945 and 1950, the average real wage of teenagers increased at twice the adult rate. Teds thus certainly had money to spend and, because it was practically all they had, it assumed a *crucial* importance. Much of the money went on clothes . . . the bootlace tie; the thick creped suede shoes; skintight, drainpipe trousers (without turnups); straighter, less-waisted jackets; moleskin or satin collars to the jackets; and the addition of vivid colours.
>
> . . . I see this choice of uniform **as**, initially, an attempt to buy status (since the clothes chosen were originally worn by upper-class dandies) . . . its symbolic cultural meaning for the Teds becomes explicable as both an expression of their social reality (basically outsiders and forced to live by their wits) and their social aspirations (basically an attempt to gain high, albeit grudging, status for an ability to live smartly, hedonistically and by their wits in an urban setting).

A famous account of the meanings behind London skinhead cultural preoccupations is summarised by Mike O'Donnell (1985):

> Phil Cohen explains the skinheads' aggressive, anti-immigrant 'territorially' defensive behaviour in the context of the decline of East End working-class communities. 'In reality', they could not reconstruct what was being lost but, in John Clarke's phrase, they performed a 'magical recovery of community' by their behaviour. In one of the most brilliant (because once stated, quite obvious) Marxist-inspired semiological interpretations, Cohen decodes their 'uniform'

Doc Marten boots, braces, collarless shirts and cropped hair – as a dramatized, exaggerated version of traditional, male, working-class attire.

In a final CCCS example, Dick Hebdige (1979) translates Rastafarian culture:

Clothed in dreadlocks and 'righteous ire', the Rastaman effects a spectacular resolution of the material contradictions which oppress and define the West Indian community. He deciphers 'sufferation', that key term in the expressive vocabulary of ghetto culture, naming its historical causes (colonialism, economic exploitation) and promising deliverance through exodus to 'Africa'. He is the living refutation of Babylon (contemporary capitalist society), refusing to deny his stolen history. By a perverse and wilful transformation, he turns poverty and exile into 'signs of grandeur', tokens of his own esteem, tickets which will take him home to Africa and Zion when Babylon is overthrown.

In all these analyses, a particular relation between theory and method is apparent. An interest in the connections between structure and culture requires an understanding of structural features – class, gender and ethnic relations in capitalism in the case of these examples – and a comprehensive ethnographic knowledge of forms of cultural representation located (constituted) in ways of dressing, speaking and acting. But this ethnographic knowledge is not sufficient to speak for itself; its symbolic meaning can only be understood by a sociologist able to make the right connections between cultural symbols and social structure.

## POST-STRUCTURALIST RESEARCH

An interest in linguistic or discursive forms of representation is, of course, characteristic of post-structuralism. However, for the post-structuralist, the analysis of language is not a matter of getting things 'right' or revealing the 'truth'. In this tradition linguistic symbols are not imbued with meaning by knowledgeable actors, nor are they rendered meaningful by experts using theoretical and semiological analysis. Instead, things work the other way round; both the actor and the expert are constituted by the language they choose to use, so that the idea that any human subject can disclose 'reality' or the 'truth' via linguistic discourse is nonsense.

The difference between the semiological and post-structuralist positions in this respect is apparent in Sylvia Walby's (1990) comments on a decoding of feminist images by Janice Winship (1987). Winship argues that some contemporary depictions of women in advertisements represent a form of symbolic resistance to male dominance, as in one portrayal of 'streetwise' models dressed in a combination of alluring underwear, overcoats and heavy shoes, set in a street strewn with rubbish. From a post-structuralist viewpoint, however, such an interpretation cannot be deemed to be 'objectively' authentic. As Walby says, it is wrong to assume that there is only *one* meaning in such a text:

> It is more appropriate to consider that there are a number of possible readings to be constructed in the relationship between the text and its viewer . . . Different audiences bring a range of experiences to the viewing and thus interpret the text differently, producing various meanings.

Unlike the cultural analyst employing semiological techniques then, the post-structuralist denies that *any* human interpreter of discourse can claim to have got its meanings 'right'. The work of Frenchman Jacques Derrida is the best-known (and most controversial) example of this post-structuralist project.

For the post-structuralist, identity and reality are constituted by discourse. Discourses are ways of representing the world, and when they take a physical form they usually do so as the languages and images used in texts. Most post-structuralist research therefore takes the form of textual analysis. The point to remember, however – and it is one that can be difficult to grasp (or accept) – is that post-structuralists do not see the *authors* of texts creating the representations of reality they produce. Just as our identities are not our creation – they are created by our implication in the variety of discourses we encounter and are obliged to use – so the world as it is portrayed through a text is not the *invention* of the writer, but is the creation of the language he or she chooses to use.

Thus, the dilemma for authors – whether scientists or novelists, advertisers or film-makers, philosophers or sociologists – who would claim to be able to correctly depict reality is this: since, as humans, we *have* to use language to portray the world, both to ourselves and to others, as soon as we do, we necessarily lose control over the meanings our account conveys because language produces meaning for us. Because we have to say whatever we *intend* to say using language, we can never be in charge of what we *end up* by saying. Thus, *deconstruction*, as Derrida calls it, is always necessary to discover the meaning in texts, even though these deconstructive efforts, as texts in themselves, can in turn only be understood by their *own* deconstruction by others, and then *their* accounts by other's deconstruction, and so on, ad infinitum. This is why a true account of reality via discursive depiction is an impossibility.

Such relativism is thus the curse of being human. Ethnomethodologists deny the possibility of *members* making objective sense of social situations because we are hampered by our own subjectivity. Kuhn denies that *scientists* can objectively reveal reality, because of their implication in socially constructed paradigms, and Foucault denies that *subjects* can create their own identities. Because post-structuralists in the style of Derrida deny that human beings can interpret reality except in discursive ways, they argue that immediately these are used, they inevitably create the potential for interpretation by others in ways unintended by the user. Thus, though there may be truth, it cannot be understood or depicted by human beings, who *must* always be users of, and therefore powerless in the face of, discourse. However, a recognition of this inevitable relativism does not, of course, excuse the post-structuralist the obligation to make available his or her *personal* deconstructive account.

## Feminist post-structuralism

Research by feminist post-structuralists provides a good example of deconstruction in practice. Part of the project for feminist post-structuralists is similar to that for Black feminists – to oppose essentialism (the idea that the meaning of womanhood is the same for women everywhere) – and to reveal the variety and elusiveness of the different forms which femininity, or 'being a woman' can take. For the feminist post-structuralist, because the meaning of the term 'woman' is differently constructed in different discourses, the researcher's job is to retrieve the respective meanings he or she personally finds in the rubble created by the deconstruction of these discourses. As Sylvia Walby (1990) puts it: 'The project for many feminist post-structuralists is to explore the variety of forms of femininity and masculinity. The substantive focus is usually an investigation of the forms of representation of gender in cultural texts such as film, literature, magazines and pictures. Such writers try to catch the nuances of different forms of femininity . . .'

For the feminist post-structuralist, however, this sort of *description* of the variety of forms of representation contained in texts (by both word and image) is not enough. Following Foucault's lead they also want to know about their political, or power, dimension. The question is: who benefits from this form of representation?

For the feminist post-structuralist, the answer is clear. Just as radical feminists point to the way in which discourses about 'normal sexuality' allow men to use heterosexual, penetrative, sex to exploit, and exercise control over women (see pp. 78–80), so feminist post-structuralists argue a similar case about discourses concerning the female body. For them, women are just as exploited by feeling the need to aspire to elusive bodily images; the contemporary discursive pressure on Western women to engage in a lifelong pursuit of slenderness is the obvious example. Though today Western males are also under some pressure to 'watch their weight' this is as nothing compared to the bombardment which their female counterparts experience concerning the 'body beautiful'. Historically, different discourses prevailed; for example, Rubens' female figures glory in their voluptuousness and physical substance. Cross-culturally too, other theories of the female body beautiful demand allegiance; for example, in some tribal societies today, girls are systematically fattened before entering womanhood via marriage.

In the West however, youth and slenderness are promoted ceaselessly as constituting the ideal, with huge financial benefits for the slimming industry. From this point of view, the 'illnesses' of anorexia and bulimia, while obviously indicating psychological torment, should not be seen as *ir*rational. Just as radical feminists see male violence towards women not so much as the acts of perverted minds but as the inevitable consequence of the public discursive representation of women, in text and image, as compliant playthings awaiting male pleasure (see p. 80), so feminist post-structuralists see anorexia and bulimia as equally inevitable, socially constructed, consequences of the relentless discursive pressure females feel to 'shape up'.

However, other feminist sociologists reject the post-structuralist view of the woman as a helpless, de-centred subject whose identity and existence is buffeted this way and that by the sea-changes wrought by different discourses. For them, women who are empowered with the right knowledge have the chance to chart their own progress through the waters of life, and sociology should be an instrument which they can use to do it.

## FEMINIST RESEARCH: SOCIAL RESEARCH AS A POLITICAL PROJECT

For such feminists, traditional sociology has failed women, and they argue that there is a need for exclusively women-oriented research, concerning itself with the kinds of issues and problems which only women experience. Justifying research with this deliberate bias is easy for such feminists, since for them most other research is what they call 'malestream' – preoccupied with investigating the world that men inhabit, but paying little attention to that lived in by women.

Such gender-specific research should, it is often argued, use methods which allow women to speak for themselves. Although women researchers should make use of their own experiences (since, as women, they are part of their subject-matter), this should not in any way mean that such research is expert-centred, in a positivist fashion, involving the investigation of the hunches and hypotheses of the specialist sociological theorist.

The purpose of feminist research should be the *political* one of giving women the voice they are normally denied in everyday life; such research should therefore use interpretive, anti-positivist research procedures generating qualitative data, with the aim of liberating and articulating the world views, perceptions and theories of women as subjects. Any pursuit of neutrality, in order to retain the objectivity so beloved of twentieth-century positivism, must therefore be rejected in favour of the deliberate production of research data to aid women's liberation. Like feminist theorising then, feminist research should have the explicitly political aim of advancing the cause of women's emancipation from oppression, by securing structural changes to patriarchal societies.

The fundamentally political nature of feminist research means that the normal 'malestream' relationship between researcher and subjects of research should be jettisoned in favour of a self-conscious attempt to make the research a collaboration *between* women, *for* women. Some feminists refer to the malestream researcher-subject relationship as the 'research as rape' model: as Shulamit Reinharz (1983) describes it: 'Conducted on a rape model, the researchers take, hit and run. They intrude into their subjects' privacy, disrupt their perceptions, utilise false pretences, manipulate the relationships, and give little or nothing in return. When the needs of the researchers are satisfied, they break off contact with the subjects.'

Even when this form of exploitation is avoided by regarding the research as an exercise in women's collaboration, however, there are still pressures encouraging the woman researcher to disengage from a proper involvement with her subjects, which some researchers find irresistible. Foremost among these is the desire to persuade others – such as funding bodies and academic colleagues, for example – of the validity of her results. The researcher can do everything right – researching women, asking questions about women's lives, using interpretive methods to allow women a voice, and so on – except when it comes to making public her political commitment to the feminist cause. Afraid that such a demonstration of partisanship will tarnish her data (and reputation) in the eyes of others in malestream sociology, the researcher fails to declare her interest and betrays her fellow women by adopting a self-consciously neutral, distanced detachment.

What of the counter-argument to this, that politically committed, collaborative and partisan data-collection procedures will simply mean that malestream sociology rejects the findings as inevitably subjective, and amounting only to prejudice dressed up as research? The usual feminist response to this echoes Howard Becker's justification of interactionist research taking such an interest in the world view of deviants. Becker extols the virtues of side-taking, or partisanship, in research – the deliberate concentration on the circumstances of the labelled and the powerless ('society's underdogs', as he calls them), and the description of the world as seen through their eyes – on the grounds that this simply goes a small way towards rectifying the gross imbalance which nearly always otherwise prevails in sociology, where the world is depicted from the other side – from the point of view of society's advantaged and powerful overdogs. As Goffman (1968) puts it in his preface to *Asylums*:

> To describe the patients' situation faithfully is necessarily to present a partisan view. (For this last bias I partly excuse myself by arguing that the imbalance is at least on the right side of the scale, since almost all professional literature on mental patients is written from the point of view of the psychiatrist, and he, socially speaking, is on the other side.)

In similar fashion, other standpoint feminists, such as Abbott and Wallace (1990) argue, in quasi-Weberian fashion, that since *all* depictions of reality are selective and partial, and since the selection is routinely male-biased in malestream sociology, all they are doing is rectifying *this* imbalance. Furthermore, their argument goes:

> . . . men's knowledge can never be complete. It is not just that the oppressed can see more, but also that their knowledge emerges through their struggle against oppression – women's knowledge emerges from a struggle against men and the attempt to replace the distorted knowledge produced by men which is used to control and subordinate women . . . Feminist science is better able to reflect the world as it is and is able to replace the distorted and distorting accounts produced by malestream sociology . . .

## POSTSCRIPT

So, where does this litany of debate and dispute in theorising and research in sociology leave us? At least we are now in a position to ask appropriate questions. For example, as human beings, are we creative agents, writing our own life-stories? Or are we constituted subjects, whose destinies are dictated by biographical forces outside our control? If so, how should we make sense of such forces? Are they normative, material, cultural, discursive or what? Or is human life best understood from both structural *and* action viewpoints – as a time when, though we *can* try to be who *we* want to be, we nevertheless do so in structural circumstances not of our choosing?

Furthermore, how should we acquire knowledge of social life? Should we embrace science, reject it, or see the construction of scientific knowledge as itself a process requiring sociological understanding? Can the knowledge we acquire be judged true or false, or is human understanding inevitably relative – a product of a time and place? If so, should we dispense with the search for 'truth' altogether? The answers to these kinds of questions may be elusive, but the obligation to look for them is not just a price we have to pay for being human. It is also a privilege no other living thing can enjoy.

# Bibliography

Abbott, P. and Wallace, C. 1990. *An Introduction to Sociological Theory: Feminist Perspectives*. London: Routledge and Kegan Paul.

Anderson, R. 1979. Listening to conversation. In R. Meighan, I. Shelton and T. Marks (eds), *Perspectives on Society*. Sunbury-on-Thames: Nelson.

Ariès, P. 1973. *Centuries of Childhood*. Harmondsworth: Penguin.

Atkinson J. M. 1977. Coroners and the categorisation of deaths as suicide. In C. Bell and H. Newby (eds), *Doing Sociological Research*. London: Allen and Unwin.

Badham, R. 1986. *Theories of Industrial Society*. London: Croom Helm.

Barker, E. 1981. *The Professional Stranger*. Milton Keynes: Open University Press.

Barker, E. 1986. *Making of a Moonie: Choice or Brainwashing?* Oxford: Basil Blackwell.

Becker, H. *et al.* 1963. *Boys in White*. Chicago: Chicago University Press.

Becker, H. 1970. *Sociological Work*. New Brunswick: Transaction Books.

Beynon, H. 1973. *Working for Ford*. Harmondsworth: Penguin.

Bilton, T. *et al.* 1987. *Introductory Sociology*. Basingstoke: Macmillan.

Bloor, D. 1984. A sociological theory of objectivity. In S. C. Brown (ed.) *Objectivity and Cultural Divergence*. Cambridge: Cambridge University Press.

Bouchier, D. 1983. *The Feminist Challenge*. Basingstoke: Macmillan.

Cheal, D. 1991. *Family and the State of Theory*. Hemel Hempstead: Harvester Wheatsheaf.

Craib, I. 1984. *Modern Social Theory*. Hemel Hempstead: Harvester Wheatsheaf.

Cuff, E. C., Payne, G. *et al.* 1979. *Perspectives in Sociology*. London: Allen and Unwin.

Cuff, E. C., Francis, D. W. and Sharrock, W. W. 1990. *Perspectives in Sociology* (3rd edition). London: Unwin Hyman.

Douglas, J. D. 1967. *The Social Meanings of Suicide*. Princeton: Princeton University Press.

Doyal, L. and Harris, R. 1986. *Empiricism, Explanation and Rationality*. London: Routledge and Kegan Paul.

Durkheim, E. 1938. *The Rules of Sociological Method*. Chicago: University of Chicago Press.

Durkheim, E. 1970. *Suicide*. London: Routledge and Kegan Paul.

Durkheim, E. 1974. *Sociology and Philosophy*. New York: Free Press.

Durkheim, E. 1976. *The Elementary Forms of Religious Life*. London: Allen and Unwin.

Feyerabend, P. 1981. Philosophical Papers, Vol II, *Problems of Empiricism*. Cambridge: Cambridge University Press.

Filmer, P. *et al.* 1972. *New Directions in Sociological Theory*. London: Collier-Macmillan.

Garfinkel, H. 1967. *Studies in Ethnomethodology*. Englewood Cliffs: Prentice-Hall.

Giddens, A. 1987. *Social Theory and Modern Sociology*. Cambridge: Polity.

Goffman, E. 1968. *Asylums*. Harmondsworth: Penguin.

Goffman, E. 1969. *The Presentation of Self in Everyday Life*. Harmondsworth: Penguin.

Hall, S. and Jefferson, T. 1976. *Resistance through Ritual*. London: Hutchinson.

Hartmann, H. 1981. The unhappy marriage of Marxism and feminism: towards a more progressive union. In L. Sargent (ed.) *Women and Revolution*. London: Pluto Press.

Hebdige, D. 1979. *Subculture: the Meaning of Style*. London: Methuen.

Kuhn, T. S. 1962. *The Structure of Scientific Revolutions* Chicago: University of Chicago Press.

Layder, D. *et al.* 1991. The empirical correlates of action and structure: the transition from school to work. *Sociology* 25:3: August 1991.

Lee, D. and Newby, H. 1983. *The Problem of Sociology*. London: Hutchinson.

Lemert, E. 1967. *Human Deviance, Social Problems and Social Control*. Englewood Cliffs: Prentice-Hall.

Lupton, T. 1963. *On the Shop Floor*. Oxford: Pergamon Press.

Mair, L. 1972. *An Introduction to Social Anthropology*. Oxford: Clarendon.

Malinowski, B. 1922. *Argonauts of the Western Pacific*. London: Routledge and Kegan Paul.

Marx, K. and Engels, F. 1976. *Collected Works*. London: Lawrence and Wishart.

Maynard, M. 1989. *Sociological Theory*. Harlow: Longman.

Newby, H. *et al.* 1984. *The British Questionnaire: the International Project on Class Structure and Class Consciousness*. British Project, Technical Paper 3. University of Essex Department of Sociology.

Newby, H. 1977. *The Deferential Worker*. London: Allen Lane.

O'Donnell, M. 1985. *Age and Generation*. London: Tavistock.

Parkin, F. 1982. *Max Weber*. London: Tavistock.
Parsons, T. 1966. *Societies: Evolutionary and Comparative Perspectives*. Englewood Cliffs: Prentice-Hall.
Parsons, T. 1971. *The System of Modern Societies*. Englewood Cliffs: Prentice-Hall.

*Red Stockings Manifesto* 1979. New York: Red Stockings Press.
Reinharz, S. 1983. Experiential analysis: a contribution to feminist research. In G. Bowles and R. D. Klein (eds), *Theories of Women's Studies*. London: Routledge and Kegan Paul.

Sacks, H. 1967. The search for help: no-one to turn to. In E. S. Schneidman (ed.), *Essays in Self-destruction*. New Jersey: Science House.
Schutz, A. 1967. Collected Papers, Vol. 1. *The Problem of Social Reality*. Amsterdam: Martinus Nijhoff.
Sharrock, W. W. 1977. The problem of order. In P. Worsley (ed.), *Introducing Sociology*. Harmondsworth: Penguin.
*Social Studies Review*, September 1990. Oxford: Philip Allan Publishers.
Stanko, E. 1985. *Intimate Intrusions*. London: Routledge and Kegan Paul.

Thomas, W. I. 1966. In M. Janowitz (ed.), *Organization and Social Personality: Selected Papers*. Chicago: University of Chicago Press.
Trigg, R. 1985. *Understanding Social Science*. Oxford: Basil Blackwell.

Uberoi, J. Singh. 1962. *The Politics of the Kula Ring*. Manchester: Manchester University Press.

Walby, S. 1990. *Theorizing Patriarchy*. Oxford: Basil Blackwell.
Wallis, R. 1983. In M. Mann (ed.) *The Macmillan Student Encyclopaedia of Sociology*. Basingstoke: Macmillan.
Weber, M. 1949. *The Methodology of the Social Sciences*. New York: Free Press.
Weber, M. 1977. *The Protestant Ethic and the Spirit of Capitalism*, London: Allen and Unwin.
Weber, M. 1949. *Economy and Society*. California: University of California Press.
Whyte, W. F. 1943. *Street Corner Society*, Chicago: University of Chicago Press.
Willis, P. 1977. *Learning to Labour*. Westmead: Saxon House.
Winch, P. 1970. *The Idea of a Social Science*. London: Routledge and Kegan Paul.
Winship, J. 1987. *Inside Women's Magazines*. London: Pandora.
Wittgenstein, L. 1973. *Philosophical Investigations*. Oxford: Basil Blackwell.

# INDEX